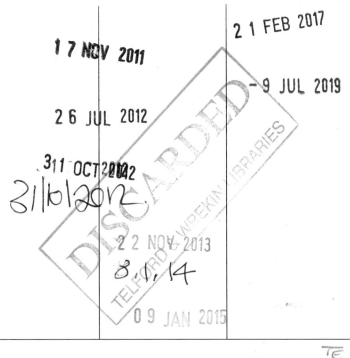
Please return/renew this item
by the last date shown.
Books may also be renewed by
phone and Internet

Telford and Wrekin **Libraries**

About the Author

Chiz's cycle touring adventures almost happened by accident, when after a local photography trip by bike she realised that she'd done 50 miles in a single day with a reasonably heavy load. This lead to the disconnected logic that if she could do that once, she was now ready to tackle serious multi-day cycle touring, and two weeks later set out on the Land's End to John o'Groats route!

Since then she's done several other multi-day trips including cycling the entire Welsh coastline (600 miles and 16km of ascent) but still maintains that you don't need to be seriously fit or fast to enjoy long multi-day routes. (She certainly makes no claim to being either!) She has also recently won the OWPG award for her photography.

Chiz had great fun re-riding some old favourites in the Peak and also discovering some completely new routes for this guidebook, and hopes you have as much fun exploring them as she did while researching them for the book.

CYCLING IN THE PEAK DISTRICT

by Chiz Dakin

2 POLICE SQUARE, MILNTHORPE, CUMBRIA LA7 7PY
www.cicerone.co.uk

© Chiz Dakin 2011
ISBN: 978 1 85284 630 5
First edition 2011

Printed by MCC Graphics, Spain.
A catalogue record for this book is
available from the British Library.

All photographs are by the author

Acknowledgements

To Reuben, for your patience,
support and love. Without you, this
book may not have made it off the
starting line and your help in route
testing has been invaluable.

Many thanks also to the CTC and
Sustrans for their help in resolving
the footpaths issue; Alastair of
Yorkshire Water for his help in
getting permission to include the
Ewden track as a concessionary
path for cycles in this guidebook;
Rob and Emily of the National Trust
for their help in making the routes
across Bobus Moor and through
Lyme Park practical. And last but not
least to Andy, and various members
of the Oread Mountaineering
Club (especially John), for help
with additional route testing/being
willing models for the camera and
staying enthusiastic even in very wet
conditions!

Advice to Readers

Readers are advised that, while
every effort is made by our
authors to ensure the accuracy of
guidebooks as they go to print,
changes can occur during the
lifetime of an edition. Please
check the Cicerone website
(www.cicerone.co.uk) for any
updates before planning your
trip. It is also advisable to check
information on such things as
transport, accommodation and
shops locally. Even rights of way can
be altered over time. We are always
grateful for information about any
discrepancies between a guidebook
and the facts on the ground, sent by
email to info@cicerone.co.uk or by
post to Cicerone, 2 Police Square,
Milnthorpe LA7 7PY.

Front cover: A pleasant late
afternoon's cycle near Middleton-
by-Youlgrave (Route 8)

CONTENTS

INTRODUCTION 9
Geology 10
Wildlife 12
Plants and flowers 13
History 15
Art, culture and local festivities. 16
Getting there 17
Money 18
Getting around. 18
When to go 18
Accommodation. 19
Food and drink. 20
What to wear 21
What to take. 23
Maps 24
Emergencies and first aid 24
Waymarking and access 25
Using this guide 28

THE ROUTES
1 Chesterfield Loop via Transpennine Trail 33
2 Carsington Reservoir Loop 38
3 Ashopton Loop via Derwent Reservoir 43
4 Middlewood Loop via Lyme Park 48
5 Bamford Loop via Ladybower Reservoir 54
6 Ashbourne Loop via Hognaston 59
7 Chesterfield Loop via Holymoorside and Leash Fen 64
8 Tissington Loop via Elton 70
9 Wirksworth Loop via Hartington 77
10 Bakewell Loop via Hartington 84
11 Leek Loop via the Roaches. 90
12 Waterhouses Loop via Morridge and Longnor 97
13 Penistone Loop via Holmfirth. 104
14 Tideswell Loop via Peak Forest. 110
15 Buxton Loop via Bakewell 117
16 Grindleford Loop via Edale 126

17 Bamford Loop via Mam Tor 135
18 Middlewood Loop via Pym Chair. 143
19 Marsden Loop via Saddleworth Moor. 150
20 Macclesfield Loop via the Roaches 158

21 Tour de Peak District 166
    Day 1   Matlock to Dungworth 167
    Day 2   Dungworth to Marsden 175
    Day 3   Marsden to Whaley Bridge 183
    Day 4   Whaley Bridge to Blackshaw Moor 193
    Day 5   Blackshaw Moor to Matlock 200

APPENDIX A Cycle hire 208
APPENDIX B Cycles and trains. 211
APPENDIX C Car parking 213
APPENDIX D Repair guide 215
APPENDIX E Route summary table. 218

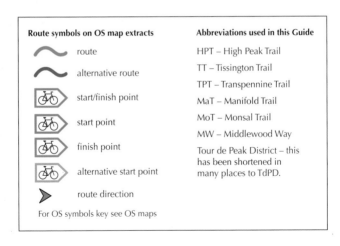

Route symbols on OS map extracts

route

alternative route

start/finish point

start point

finish point

alternative start point

route direction

For OS symbols key see OS maps

Abbreviations used in this Guide

HPT – High Peak Trail

TT – Tissington Trail

TPT – Transpennine Trail

MaT – Manifold Trail

MoT – Monsal Trail

MW – Middlewood Way

Tour de Peak District – this
has been shortened in
many places to TdPD.

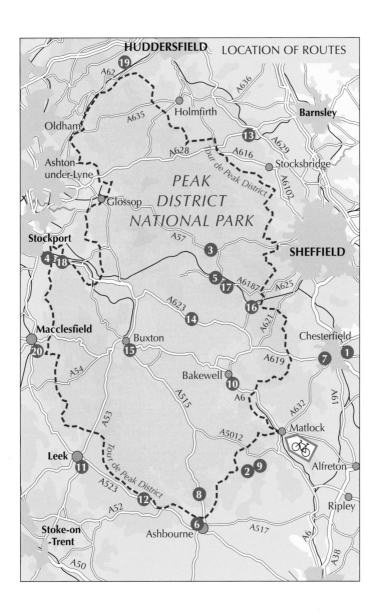

Monsal Viaduct in spring (Route 15)

INTRODUCTION

Cycling around a bend on a narrow moorland lane above Hathersage, I stopped briefly at a wider space on the lane to write up some notes from the route I was recceing. I'd only written a few words when the friend I was cycling with whispered quietly 'Chiz, look over there – there's a curlew on the ground!' Quietly I dropped my pen and paper and shuffled over to the drystone wall, hoping that any movement I made was hidden by the wall. Peeking over, not only was there one curlew, but three, and they seemed to be in some sort of dispute – perhaps two males vying for the attention of a female!

They were much larger than I'd imagined – previously having only ever heard them in the sky above – and by staying low by the drystone wall we were treated to a display of low-flying acrobatics for several minutes. Eventually one flew away over the fields below, one landed on the moorland nearby and one disappeared into long grass at the far end of the field. Such encounters are not common, but when they happen are all the more special for their rarity – had we been in a car, we'd have whizzed past so fast we'd never have even seen the first curlew; walking, we'd probably have disturbed them with our movement before we got close.

But cycling is the perfect way to experience the countryside – fast

Cyclists on a track shortly after the road end, Derwent Reservoir (Route 3)

enough to cover a good distance over the ground, yet slow enough to really enjoy the sights, sounds and (mostly!) the smells of the countryside. From the pungent aroma of wild garlic, the swathes of bluebells that carpet the floor of many woodlands in spring, the haunting cry of the curlew or joyful tweet of the skylark, to the purple blush of vetch in summer or flowering moorland heather in early autumn: on a bicycle the variety of the landscape can be appreciated in both detail and grander scale.

The Peak District needs no introduction to many – it has a string of firsts and mosts in England and the UK to its credit. It was the first National Park to be created in 1959, it's the most central National Park and the nearest wild outdoor space to the largest percentage of the population. Its 'Wonders' were first eulogised over by William Camden in the 16th century in *Britannia* (the first topographical and historical survey of Britain) and it is now one of the most popular National Parks in the UK.

While the honeypots of Castleton, Bakewell and Dovedale can get very busy at the height of summer they can soon be left behind on the quiet lanes and tracks that criss-cross this wonderfully varied region. This guidebook aims to introduce the reader to some of these wonderful routes, covering between 15km (10 miles) and 60km (37 miles) in a day, and leading up to a finale – the multi-day Tour de Peak District – a new five-day route running roughly around the edge of this fantastic region and within the grasp of anyone of average fitness.

GEOLOGY

The Peak District was once a shallow tropical sea, and cyclists may find it hard to believe that 350 million years ago, the land they are riding over was once close to the Equator and completely underwater (perhaps that'll be more believable to those visiting on a dull wet day!). Fringed by coral reefs and sea lilies (crinoids) with shellfish swimming around, the calcium carbonate of their remains went on to form limestone.

Later on (325–300 million years ago) the tropical sea slowly drained away when a huge river delta to the north advanced slowly southwards. This river delta dropped first mud, then coarser layers of sand and grits, today known as gritstone.

These two types of rock – limestone and gritstone – are the constituents of the Peak District. The differences in colour and the distinctive separation of the two types of rock – roughly gritstone to the north and western and eastern fringes, and limestone in the central and southern areas – lead to the popular names of 'White Peak' and 'Dark Peak' for the southern limestone and northern gritstone regions respectively. Gritstone is sometimes also called millstone grit due its long-standing use for millstones.

There is also a third, lesser known, type of rock – an area of shale, formed from the early mud layers deposited by the encroaching river delta. This is often exposed on the boundary between the older limestone and more recent gritstone – the 'shivering mountain' of Mam Tor (Route 17) is a good example of this intermediate layer.

More recently (geologically speaking) the region was lifted and folded to form a gentle dome. Overlying deposits of coal were worn away (eroded), followed by some of the gritstone and shales, revealing the weaker limestone beneath the higher parts of the region. Being weaker, this limestone has eroded more quickly,

Abandoned millstones at Lawrencefield – a common use for gritstone, hence its alternative name 'millstone grit'

The 'shivering mountain' of Mam Tor – on the line of shale deposits (Route 17)

11

leaving behind gritstone edges such as Froggatt, Stanage (Route 16) and Windgather Rocks (Route 18).

WILDLIFE

There is a surprising variety of animals to be seen in Derbyshire and the Peak District. Aside from the ubiquitous Derbyshire sheep, llamas, ostriches and alpacas are farmed at many locations across the region. Wilder creatures such as deer, foxes and rabbits are all frequently seen, but an absence of loud footsteps can also reward you with glimpses of startled stoats and even adders.

Other less common sightings are of mountain hares and red-necked wallabies. The original group of wallabies escaped into the wild from a private zoo near the Roaches (Routes 11, 18, 20) in the late 1940s. Their descendants were thought to have become extinct around 2000, but recent sightings in the Roaches and Buxton areas suggest otherwise. At least one yak also escaped at the same time – last seen on the moorlands in 1951, so probably yaks are no longer part of Peak District wildlife – but like Scottish wildcats, you never know! However, just south of the Peak District near Derby,

(Top to bottom) Curlew flying over Bamford Moor (Route 16); The bright yellow siskin can frequently be seen near the River Derwent; Finches, like this chaffinch, are a common sight.

passers-by can often see a friendly water-buffalo in the fields (he's called Oink – having grown up with pigs he learned to imitate their sounds).

Nearer water or hay meadows, dragonflies and all sorts of butterflies are frequently sighted. More rarely, water voles can sometimes be seen beside streams, and apparently the strange sucker-mouthed river lamphrey exist in our waterways (sighted usually only by experts).

Any cyclist interested in birdlife will find the Peak District a fantastic location, with a wide abundance of species, from the tiny goldcrest, the redstart and the brightly coloured siskin; to curlews, buzzards and geese. Kestrels are frequently seen hovering over fields and moorlands, waiting to pounce on unsuspecting small mammals. Grouse are a common sight and sound on the moorlands, but more common still is the pleasant warble of the skylark, high above the ground; lower down, the weaving acrobatics of swallows also provide entertainment.

In the vales and dales, dippers are often seen bobbing alongside limestone streams. Ducklings are also a very common sight in early–mid summer; stonechats (named for their distinctive call which sounds like small stones knocking together) are often seen, finches of all descriptions are highly common and the lucky viewer may get to see a kingfisher along the banks of the River Derwent. On the reservoirs and other larger bodies of water, geese are nearly always honking on Ladybower (Route 5) and over winter lapwings grace Carsington Water (Route 2).

PLANTS AND FLOWERS

The purple blush of moorland heather turning the harsh upland landscape into a much softer and more colourful scene needs no introduction to anyone who has seen tourist brochure images of the Peak District: this is best seen in late July to early September.

While snowdrops are often the first to flower, it's March before more wild flowers are in evidence, with daffodils being among the first (Route 19 has a surprisingly good display up the hill to Wessenden Moor). Soon after that bluebells form carpets of blue for a few brief spring weeks (Grenoside woods, just north of Sheffield, is a good place to see these), and wild garlic often goes rampant, creating pungent swathes of white – both bluebells and wild garlic prefer limestone woodlands.

Come late spring/early summer, many fields explode into flower as the hay meadows take advantage of increasing sunshine (yes, Derbyshire really does get some!) and one of the Peak District's many rare species – the early purple orchid – comes into flower. A short detour into one of many of the limestone dales will be rewarded with a view of this small purple flower: Monks Dale (near

Derbyshire bluebells

Route 15) is especially renowned for them. Meanwhile hawthorn trees create a profusion of white-flowered hedges.

Later on, the verges of many country lanes gain an infusion of pink (from rosebay willowherb, foxgloves, campion), blue–purple

(Below, left to right) Snowdrops are one of the earliest flowers to appear; Bluebell stems beginning to flower; Early purple orchid (Route 14).

Rosebay willowherb – a very common summer flower in the limestone parts of the Peak District

(vetch, cranesbill and harebells – especially towards Staffordshire/Cheshire), white (cow parsley and daisies of all sizes) or yellow (from humble dandelions and buttercups to poisonous ragwort). Many of the rough upland moorlands also turn shimmering white with cotton grass.

From August onwards, purple-stained fingers and lips give away those who have been enjoying the deliciously ripe wild bilberries (moorlands) and brambles (lower-lying lands); but nettles, brambles, bracken and butterbur (huge rhubarb-like leaves lining limestone dales) threaten to take over any path not frequently ridden.

Autumn then brings beautiful leafy shades of red, yellow and brown – especially beech and chestnut trees, whose nuts are now ripe and falling before winter claims a harsh quietness in the floral world and the cycle starts once again in January.

HISTORY

Cyclists would be forgiven for thinking the Peak District was named for its abundance of hilly routes, but in fact this has nothing to do with topography, and everything to do with an ancient tribe called the *Paec*. These *Paec-saetna* were Anglo-Saxons from further south, who moved up the Dove and Derwent valleys and settled in what became known as the Peak District from roughly AD400. Over time they became a distinctly separate tribe from their southern, lowland cousins and the term *Paec-saetna* (or Pec-saetan) was used to distinguish them from other dark-age

15

inhabitants of Mercia. (At this time England was divided into three kingdoms: Mercia formed the middle kingdom between Northumberland and Wessex.) The regional name of 'Peak District' is thought to come directly from this ancient 'Paec' tribe.

Going back much further in time, Creswell Crags is the furthest north site known to have been inhabited before the last glaciation: the site offers signs that nomadic hunter gatherers reached the Peak District between 45,000 and 10,000BC.

More recently, many of the fringes of the Peak District were hotbeds of industrial revolution – with Richard Arkwright's Mills giving the Derwent Valley UNESCO World Heritage status, and the Platt brothers of Saddleworth's cotton-spinning technology a less well known but highly important part of the industrial history of the region. Railways blossomed, and industrial extraction of raw materials shaped the landscape as we see it today.

ART, CULTURE AND LOCAL FESTIVITIES

The Peak District is a thriving region for artists and craft-workers of all disciplines. The Arts Derbyshire website (www.artsderbyshire.com) is a good place to start looking for information on what's going on. Alternatively local magazines such as *Derbyshire Life* and the *Derbyshire Times* often include information on local upcoming events. Tourist information centres in Buxton, Bakewell, Holmfirth, Leek, Matlock, Chesterfield and Macclesfield are also useful sources of information.

Derbyshire and the Peak District are also home to a number of lesser-known traditions and cultural events. Well-dressing is perhaps the best known of these, where a clay 'tablet' is pressed with flowers and other (usually natural) materials to make a picture. The 'well', as it is locally called, tends to be made by the locals of a village over the course of a week or so, and is then blessed and displayed near their water source. This custom is thought to have its origins in an ancient pagan ritual

Well-dressing at Carsington Visitor Centre (Route 2)

giving thanks for fresh water; the tradition is (almost) uniquely found in Derbyshire, although a recent revival is spreading into Staffordshire and other parts of the UK.

Other notable festivities include Shrovetide Football, a town-wide ancient game played over a 'pitch' of three miles on Shrove Tuesday and Ash Wednesday (Feb/Mar) in Ashbourne (Route 6); Garland Day in Castleton, a celebration that originated in Charles I's escape from the Roundhead army by hiding in an oak tree (29 May: Route 17); Buxton Festival, a festival with its roots in new opera, that now encompasses literature, off-beat classical music and walking (July: Route 15); Bakewell Agricultural Show (Aug; Routes 10 and 15); Wirksworth Art and Architecture Trail Festival – an unusual but highly renowned art exhibition where many of the local houses become part of a town-wide art gallery for a weekend (Sep: Route 9); and Matlock Bath Illuminations – the inland town that believes it's on the sea-front lights up the autumn (Sep/Oct: near start/end of Tour de Peak District, see Route 21).

GETTING THERE

Overseas visitors
Although there is a very good regional **airport** at East Midlands, overseas visitors to the UK (from outside Europe) are more likely to arrive by air in either London or Manchester.

From London, there is a choice of **train** from London St Pancras to Derby, Chesterfield or Sheffield (East Midlands Trains) or from London Euston to Stoke, Macclesfield and Manchester (Virgin Trains and London Midland Trains). From Manchester trains run to Sheffield, Leeds and Buxton (Northern Trains, First Transpennine Trains). Sheffield is additionally served by East Midlands Trains. Trains link back from Leeds in the NE to Birmingham in the SW via Sheffield and Derby (Cross Country). See Appendix B for more information on taking your bicycle by train.

A number of **hire car companies** operate throughout the UK. As well as the well-known large multinational chains serving the UK market, smaller operators include Holiday Autos, enterprise, premiercarjet, car hire 3000. Price comparison sites such as www.moneysupermarket. com, www.kayak.co.uk, www.opodo. co.uk and www.lastminute.com are useful when searching for a good deal at the last minute.

Visas are needed by some foreign nationals – see www.ukvisas.gov.uk/en/doineedvisa/ for more information. Short term (6-month) tourist visas usually cost roughly £70.

European visitors
Regional **airports** such as East Midlands (Derby/Nottingham/ Leicester) in the south, Leeds/

Bradford or Robin Hood (Doncaster) in the north-east, or Manchester for the north-west tend to be served by low-cost and budget airlines, and will usually provide a better gateway for European visitors than London. **Trains** running from these airports to cities near the Peak District are as detailed above, plus Doncaster to Leeds or Sheffield (Cross Country, Northern, East Coast, First Transpennine).

District (especially with regard to overnight parking). A **cycle rack** is useful for transporting bikes, especially if carrying more than one bike. These, sadly, are often not available direct from hire companies. Alternative options include taking the train, or hiring an estate car which will take bikes in the back. Families may need to factor in the cost of purchasing a rack to the cost of their holiday.

MONEY

You should be able to find a cashpoint (ATM) in most towns these days, but it is wise to have sufficient cash for an overnight stay, meal and a day's supplies (say £35–£100 depending on your budget) as many small villages do not have one and credit and debit cards are not universally accepted by smaller businesses. Visa and Mastercard are widely accepted: occasionally places may also take American Express. Purchases of less than £5 or £10 may be refused if not in cash.

GETTING AROUND

Travellers intending to use **trains** to get around should read Appendix B for more information on the various train operating companies serving the region and their requirements in relation to carrying bikes.

Drivers should read Appendix C with regard to **parking** in the Peak

WHEN TO GO

The best time to cycle in the Peak District is the summer. Days are longer, the weather is warmer (if not always sunnier!), and routes tend to be much drier and less muddy than in winter. On the downside, accommodation and transport are busier, more expensive, get booked up earlier and the honeypot centres such as Castleton and Bakewell can fill up – especially at the weekend. But just a couple of kilometres away from these, peace and quiet can be found – even in midsummer. Many festivals, such as well dressings, take place in the summer.

Late spring and early autumn can also offer great cycling – the weather is often drier and sunnier (although often windier) and the days are still reasonably long. Accommodation is cheaper and less busy, as are trains and planes, and honeypot centres, but festivals are fewer.

Family on Manifold Trail in summer (Route 11)

Winter is not recommended for the novice cyclist – conditions can feel arctic at times, trails can be much rougher and days are short. But for the experienced and prepared cyclist, winter offers a quiet, more adventurous angle to a cycling visit to the Peak District.

ACCOMMODATION

Accommodation is widely available throughout the Peak District, although many accommodation providers in more remote areas assume arrival by car, which isn't always helpful for cyclists. More remote villages may have no or just one option for accommodation.

Check in advance with various websites (see below for some useful starting places).

Good bases of a reasonable size from which to explore the Peak District are (roughly south to north):
- Ashbourne (Routes 2, 6, 8, 9, 12)
- Wirksworth (Routes 2, 6, 8, 9, Tour de Peak District (TdPD))
- Matlock (Routes 1, 2, 7, 9, 10, TdPD)
- Hartington (Routes 8, 9, 10, 11, 12)
- Bakewell or Chesterfield (Routes 1, 7, 10, 15)
- Hathersage (Routes 3, 5, 14, 15, 16, 17, 18, 20, TdPD)
- Buxton (Routes 3, 4, 5, 10, 14, 15, 16, 17, 18, 20 TdPD)
- Macclesfield or Whaley Bridge (Routes 4, 15, 18, 20, TdPD)
- Glossop or New Mills (Routes 4, 13, 15, 18, 19)
- Marsden, Meltham or Holmfirth (Routes 13, 19, TdPD)

Smaller villages with charm and more than one B&B/pub accommodation, plus a reasonable place to eat out in the evening (usually a pub), include Alstonefield, Monyash, Tideswell, Longnor, Litton, Bradwell (a quieter alternative to Castleton) and Edale.

Further information on B&Bs/ pubs with rooms can be found at:

- Visit Peak District
  www.visitpeakdistrict.com
- Cyclists' Touring Club (CTC)'s list of Cyclists Welcome accommodation, cafés and bike shops www.ctc-maps.org.uk/ cyclists_welcome
- Peak District National Park
  www.peakdistrict-nationalpark.com
- Peak District Online – an independent information portal
  www.peakdistrictonline.co.uk
- Peak District Information – another independent portal
  www.peakdistrictinformation.com.

Note Prices vary considerably - for the TdPD roughly £40ppn or less is the cut-off between 'cheaper' accommodation (marked £) and more expensive places (marked ££).

Campsites

For information on campsites, the Camping and Caravanning Club website (www.thefriendlyclub.co.uk), with its siteseeker tool, is one of the best; alternatively try www.ukcampsite.co.uk.

Youth Hostels

Try YHA – www.yha.org.uk – or the independent Hostels Guide – www.independenthostelguide.co.uk.

FOOD AND DRINK

As to be expected of such a diverse region covering several counties, the Peak District has several distinct regional specialities, many of which are only found in certain parts of the region. Visitors to Bakewell should not miss the opportunity to make their own Bakewell Pudding at the Bakewell Pudding Shop (don't make the mistake of calling it a Bakewell Tart – locally that is regarded as a highly inferior mass-produced product compared to the real thing!).

Visitors to the west of the region may find the opportunity to sample the unique taste of Staffordshire oatcakes – particularly filled with hot melted cheese. To the north (and spreading increasingly south through the region), the Yorkshire Pudding often comes in Giant form, filled with roast beef, sausages or lamb. And speaking of lamb, Derbyshire lamb is one of the region's best known specialities: on offer at many of the region's pubs and restaurants, lamb shank with rosemary washed down with a pint of real ale is a well-earned treat after a hard day's cycling.

No food and drink section would be complete without mentioning the vast array of real ales on offer in the region's large selection of pubs and inns. As well as the region-wide offerings from the Marston's Brewery (of which Pedigree is the most common), more regional treats include Stockport's Robinson's (Unicorn), mostly in the north-west of the region, and Theakston's (XB, Best) and Black Sheep beers towards the north. More local micro-breweries, such as Hartington's Whim Brewery and Peak Ales (Bakewell/Chatsworth area), can also be sampled in many pubs.

Wine aficionados are not so well-catered for with local products but Renishaw Hall (near Sheffield) held the distinction of being the most northerly vineyard between 1972 and 1986 and has produced award-winning wine more recently. Fortunately, despite the general lack of locally-grown offerings, restaurants and increasingly pubs are fairly clued up in their understanding of the best wines to import.

WHAT TO WEAR

Newcomers to cycling would be forgiven for thinking head-to-toe lycra in lurid colours is essential, to judge by the attire of some road cycling clubs. Fortunately this is not essential to your pedalling enjoyment, although there are certain items of clothing that will make your ride more comfortable and therefore more enjoyable.

Wearing a brightly coloured waterproof is a good idea

Jacket

The weather can change notoriously quickly, especially on higher ground, and a sunny day can scarily quickly become windy and wet. A light-weight, breathable and quick-drying jacket that is both windproof and waterproof will make poor weather much more bearable, and if it is in a hi-visibility colour such as yellow or orange, with reflective patches, this will make you more visible on-road to other motorists in sudden downpours or poor light. Being breathable is important to allow sweat created going uphill (or into strong winds) to escape.

Cycling shorts

Cycling specific (padded) shorts make the effort of cycling much more comfortable, particularly for

Typical Peak District view of a small farm shed and tree in a hay meadow

those new to cycling or on longer routes. These only used to be available in close-fitting lycra, but these days mountain biking versions in other fabrics can be much more stylish and loose-fitting. Many cyclists wouldn't ride without them!

Cycling gloves

These can make arms more comfortable (especially gloves with gel-filled patches) – particularly on off-road sections, where vibrations through the handlebars are more intense – and will protect fingers to some extent if you are unlucky enough to come off the bike.

Sunglasses/Shades

These are extremely useful – even on a rainy day. As well as reducing glare from bright or low sun, they also keep flying insects, mud and driving rain out of eyes. Some mountain-bikers even wear 'clear' shades on every ride, just to keep the mud out of their eyes.

Breathable upper and lower layers

Enough for the time of year, little enough not to be overburdened – this is very much a personal preference, but a spare lightweight fleece is often a good idea if setting out with minimal clothing.

Cycling shoes and SPD pedals

As you progress in your cycling, and tackle longer and harder routes, you may find that clip-in (SPD) pedals become worthwhile. As well as holding the cyclist's feet to the pedals on bouncy ground (which isn't any benefit to the terrified novice but can be helpful to the experienced) these allow the rider to pull up with the feet

(Top) Stiff-soled cycling shoes are useful......but adding SPD plates to specialist cycling shoes is best left until you're sure it's worth the outlay in money and 'getting-used-to' time (bottom).

on each revolution of the pedals as well as pushing down. This allows a more efficient use of the rider's energy – especially going uphill. But these are best left until you are sure that the cost and 'getting-used-to' time is worth the benefits, and in the meantime a pair of trainers with reasonably stiff soles is all that is needed (the stiffer the sole the better, as cycling a lot in flexible soled shoes can lead to foot problems).

Reputable cycle hire centres will usually provide you with a lock, pump and helmet free of charge. Most will also provide a small repair kit (enough to change an inner tube), but you may well have to ask for this. A lock would be a good idea if you plan to leave your cycle unattended for longer periods of time, or in larger towns. Most indoor accommodation can usually provide somewhere reasonably secure to leave a cycle overnight (but do check before you book).

Although many hire centres will encourage you to wear a helmet, there is no requirement under UK law to wear one and this is entirely up to the individual rider to decide for themselves (although it is a good idea for small children).

Toolkit
See Appendix D for more information.

Basic First Aid kit
This should be just large enough to treat the basics if one of the party comes off the bike, without being overly heavy and cumbersome. Some useful items may include:

- disinfectant wipes
- plasters (various sizes)
- antiseptic cream
- wound pads/dressings (5cm+ sizes)
- wound closure strips
- small bandage
- small tweezers
- painkillers.

Water bottles

These (1 or 2 dependent on route length) can be held in frame-mounted bottle cages.

Luggage

Although it is possible to carry day kit in a small rucksac, it is much more pleasant and comfortable to carry things in a handlebar bag, saddlebag, rear rack bag (or panniers for larger loads). Handlebar bags with a clear top pocket to carry a map can be particularly useful. All luggage should be properly and securely fitted using appropriate brackets, with panniers also requiring a rear rack. Beware of wheels becoming snagged by loose straps or floppy panniers.

MAPS

Normally, for cycling, the Ordnance Survey (OS) 1:50,000 series offers the ideal weight-to-information compromise (or if doing long-distance tours, where many 1:50,000 maps would be required, the relevant pages taken from a 1:250,000 road atlas can be preferable). However, the Peak District is such a compact area, and the OS 1:25,000 Explorer series maps 1 and 24 cover so much of the region in just two maps, that these may well be the best choice for many routes.

OS 1:25,000 Explorer series:
* 1 – Dark Peak
* 24 – White Peak
* 21 – South Pennines

* 259 – Derby and Ashbourne
* 269 – Chesterfield and Alfreton
* 277 – Rochdale and Manchester
* 288 – Bradford and Huddersfield

The Transpennine Trail maps may also be of use:
* Map 1: West – Irish Sea to Yorkshire
* Map 2: Central – Derbyshire and Yorkshire

Ordnance Survey maps can be found in good bookstores in larger towns or online, but often the relevant local sheets can be found in village stores. Transpennine Trail maps are best bought in advance over the internet.

EMERGENCIES AND FIRST AID

In a life-threatening emergency:
* **first priority:** ensure that you and the casualty are not in further danger;
* **next:** call for help (999 or 112);
* **then:** try and give whatever first aid is practical.

It is definitely a life-threatening emergency if the casualty is not breathing or is unconscious/unresponsive to their name.

The number for the emergency services is 999. This will put you through to a combined control centre for ambulance, police and fire brigade services. 112, which is

Easy terrain on a moderate route (Route 14)

commonly used across Europe, will also get you through to the emergency services. They will find it easier and quicker to get to the casualty if you can give them a good indication of whereabouts you are – a GPS location reading (in the OS maps format such as SK 123 456) can be very handy for this and what the problem is (for example: fallen off bike, hit head on kerb and is unconscious).

If you suspect the casualty has back or neck injuries do not move them unless their life is seriously threatened if they remain where they are: any movement may worsen the risk of paralysis. If you have no choice but to move them, it is important to support their head (particularly) and back (nearly as important) fully while moving them – this may well require the help of more than one additional person.

NHS Direct may be of help if the emergency is not life-threatening but still serious: ☎ 0845 4647.

For minor injuries the first aid kit (you did bring it, didn't you?) will come in handy. If there is gravel or any other object embedded in a cut that is bleeding significantly, do not press on the foreign body directly, but press at the sides of the wound to try and stem the bleeding. Then pile wound dressing on top of wound dressing with a bandage until blood flow from the wound becomes minimal, and seek help. For more minor cuts, bruises and gravel rash, plenty of antiseptic wipes, antiseptic cream, plasters and chocolate (for the casualty to eat!) should do the trick.

WAYMARKING AND ACCESS

Access control gates (A-bars) are an increasingly common sight at the starts, ends and at access points of cycle trails. These are not (as many cyclists believe) an indication that cycling is permitted, but are actually designed so that a wheelchair user can access a walking route while preventing motorised vehicles (usually off-road motorbikes) from entering the trail. That they also allow most cyclists through is a side-effect that has been put to good use by many newer cycling trails.

Waymarking signs

Many of the routes in this book make use of National Cycle Network routes (denoted as R68, R54C and so on). These are often waymarked via sticky signs on lampposts and other street furniture. Such sticky signs tend to be better at surviving the attempts of bored kids in redirecting or 'borrowing' them for other uses. Some waymarkers, however, are still the traditional metal signpost – in town centres it is important to reserve judgment, however, as they don't always remain pointing the correct direction!

Cyclists have a right of way on bridleways, restricted byways (no motorised vehicles) and byways (all vehicles also allowed). They may also have rights on routes specially designated as cycleways

Metal Sustrans National Cycle Route sign

or cyclepaths. They do not have a 'right' of way anywhere else. Concessionary bridleways allow cyclists, but (like concessionary footpaths) confer no specific 'right' of passage, and the concession can legally be withdrawn at any time by the landowner; it's rare that concessionary footpaths also allow cyclists, but not totally unknown - signs should make this obvious.

Bridleways are usually marked with a blue arrow; byways with a 'byway' sign, or sometimes a red arrow; footpaths are usually marked with a yellow arrow. Sometimes bridleways are marked with a wooden post with a blue band painted around it – this is particularly common on the Transpennine Trail (TPT). A yellow arrow is usually, but not always, an indication that cyclists may not ride. Concessionary paths (bridleways and footpaths) are often marked with a white arrow.

The situation with cycles on footpaths is rather unclear at the current time. Legally you may not ride on a footpath, yet some newer cycleways use footpaths (and are marked as footpaths too!) and many urban footpaths have become shared pedestrian/cyclist routes. In practice, if there is a sign that indicates cycles are allowed, then you should be OK. With other paths (such as the linking track across from the top of Dirtlow Rake to the country lane or across Bobus Moor), where the rights are either unclear, lost in time, or in the process of change, they might be commonly used by cycles, and cyclists are not usually seen as a problem by the landowner, and tacitly or even (rarely!) enthusiastically encouraged). But you should always approach such areas (they are marked in the route descriptions) with caution, and if challenged be prepared to dismount or deviate.

Pushing a bike on a footpath is another contested issue. There is no law prohibiting the pushing of a bike on a footpath. The Ramblers Association claims that 'a bike is not a natural accompaniment' (on a footpath), and you may hear Rights of Way officers echoing this, but the Cyclists Touring Club (CTC) maintains that this claim has only been made in a Scottish, not English, legal case and, even then was only a comment not a legal ruling. **However**, common sense also must apply – you should not try to push a bike over a narrow single-file footpath where this would clearly cause inconvenience to walkers (for example along Chee Dale – a difficult walk without the encumberance of a bike!) and no route in this book will suggest otherwise.

Quiet Lanes

These are usually narrow country lanes where motorised users are expected to realise that there will be many cyclists, walkers and horseriders. While the majority of drivers

'Quiet Lane' signpost

are courteous, not all drivers respect these signs, so continue to take care.

RoWIPs and Demonstration Towns

RoWIP is council-speak for Rights of Way Improvement Plan, and is good news for cyclists. Since 2000, the region's councils have all been required to develop and implement RoWIPs, with the result that more cyclists are gaining greater access rights to trails and bridleways. Some of these new routes, such as the Pennine Bridleway through Derbyshire, have been around for a few years but many are only very recent, such as the Thornhill Trail (see Routes 4 and 16) and the proposed upgrade of the Derwent Valley Heritage Way to full Bridleway status.

Derby was one of the first towns in England (in 2006) to gain Cycling Demonstration Town status, when Derby-based cycling organisations such as Cycle Derby gained funding to encourage more people to get involved with cycling. Demonstration Town funding has now spread to other towns, and outside urban areas; the Peak District is the first non-urban region to benefit from similar funding. In the Peak District some of this funding is being spent on the new Pedal Peak District organisation and website, but (perhaps more importantly for those of us that already know what a fantastic means of travelling the bicycle is) this is another source of funding being used to create important new off-road routes.

Over the next few years, (as long as funding cuts don't reverse the process), cyclists should expect to see many more bridleways come into existence, joining up currently 'dead-end' bridleways, filling in 'missing links' to circular and linear routes, and resolving issues where a bridleway crosses a Council boundary and one parish or county has recorded the bridleway but the other hasn't. Some of these will be upgrades of footpath to bridleway status, some will be entirely new sections of route or once private tracks coming into public use: one exciting new development proposed for the next few years is the planned extension of the Monsal Trail south

from Bakewell. This will eventually result in a route all the way from Buxton station to Matlock station, allowing much better access to the Peak District via more sustainable transport than the car.

Sadly despite the best efforts of John Grimshaw (founder of Sustrans and Project Director of this development), the full route isn't complete at the time of publishing this guidebook, although we have been promised that the Monsal Tunnels will be open before Easter 2011! Route 15 is therefore somewhat of an interim route, but we will endeavour to publish information on the new sections of route as and when it comes into existence on the ground (in the Updates section of this guide's details on the Cicerone website). It's not ideal, but I think you will agree that it really is too important a route to leave out! And on that subject, my sincere thanks go to John Grimshaw.

USING THIS GUIDE

What sort of routes?

The routes in the book are intended for anyone of average fitness or better. This is not a technical mountain-biking guidebook – there are plenty of those already out there – nor is it a leaflet describing the many totally car-free, out-and-back family-friendly trails. It is intended to fill the gap between these two – using many of the region's quiet lanes, bridleways, byways and ancient paths. Riders will need traffic sense, as the routes do use the open road, but most of the routes are suitable for families with older children who have mastered the rules of the road sufficiently to be safe in traffic.

The region has a great variety of trails available to the cyclist – from easy-going trails that use former railway lines, to narrow, winding and often hilly country lanes, to bridleways and byways that use former turnpikes and jaggers' (packhorse drovers') paths over rougher terrain. Of course, there are occasions where the only route available to cyclists is on a busy A road – in these instances the balance of quality of route, landscape around, width and nature of road are all taken into consideration as to whether the route justifies it. In most cases it doesn't, but for a rare few (for example Saddleworth Moor) the compromise is worthwhile. Every effort will be made to ensure that A road sections are downhill, keeping time on them to an absolute minimum.

Trail grading

The routes have been subjectively graded Easy, Moderate and Hard. But everyone has different opinions about what makes a route hard: is it the length of the route, or the steepness of any uphills? Perhaps it's the combined number of hills in a route, or the terrain under wheel? Perhaps it's the inclusion of an A-road

Typical terrain on an Easy route (Route 2)

– whatever its nature – or the steepness of any descents? For the purpose of this guidebook I have adopted the following approach.

Easy routes should be relatively short (no more than 25km), not overly steep and should not climb one hill after another (cumulative ascent no more than 400m). They shouldn't use A-roads at all (although they may have to cross them). Their terrain should be suitable for anyone who has never ridden off-road before, and they will use trail-type surfaces as much as possible.

Moderate routes can be longer than Easy Routes (they range from 18 to 50km), have steeper but not extremely steep ascents and more hills in general (ideally less than 1000m total ascent over the route); they may also have steep downhills. They may tackle busier roads, where

One of the types of terrain a rider will encounter on a Moderate route (TdPD2)

needed, to join up parts of a good circular route, and will encounter rougher terrain – expect some mud, loose stones, lumpy but solid surfaces or sandy patches. These rough sections will never last too long, and (in dry conditions!) the rough sections should not be unrideable to someone who has limited experience of off-road riding on surfaces other than easy-going trails.

One of the types of terrain a rider will encounter on a Hard route (Route 16)

Hard routes tend to be the longer routes in the book (ranging from 35 to 60km) and rarely have less than 1000m of ascent over the route as a whole. (The Peak District is a hilly place.) But although they edge towards mountain-biking in places, they are never out-and-out technical off-road challenges. They may contain very short sections which some cyclists will consider unrideable

Tour de Peak District. This route deserves a category of its own. Although no stage is tougher than a 'hard' route, riders should not underestimate the cumulative effect of fatigue on a multi-day route if they have never attempted one. It is recommended that riders have ridden the equivalent of all the moderate and hard routes in the guidebook before attempting such a route. At the other end of the scale, keen and experienced riders will probably wish to compress this route into a three-day challenge.

Route statistics

Each route description starts with some statistics which will help you to make your own grading judgement, given your preferences and abilities. Although most of the figures are self-explanatory, the percentages of **Trail** and **Off-Road** require some explanation.

- **Trail** means purpose-made traffic-free cycle route, generally gently graded with a smooth firm (gravel or tarmac) surface. The route descriptions often use the word 'trail' as a general term for the route, but the description should make clear which are the harder sections of 'off-road'.

- **Off-Road** is any other non-road section, which may be steeper, rougher and muddier.

Road bikes

Can the routes be ridden in wet conditions or on a road bike? You can generally assume that 'road' and 'trail' sections of route are rideable in the wet and on road bikes. However, 'off-road' sections may be more problematic. Use the percentages, and any extra information given in the text, to judge whether you will be committing yourself to a long walk before you set out. Many of the routes make extensive use of quiet lanes and easy-going trails, and as such are suitable in the wet or on a road bike.

Some route descriptions give on-road detours to avoid more awkward off-road sections, whereas a few may be simply impractical on a road bike or in wet conditions. On all surfaces, remember that braking distances are considerably extended in the wet.

Conventions and abbreviations

Sustrans National Cycle Routes are abbreviated to, for example, R68 for National Cycle Route 68 or R54 for National Cycle Route 54. This should not be confused with a route number from this guidebook, eg Route 68 (which does not exist!), but if it did would be written as Route 68.

Former railway lines now used as cycle trails are abbreviated in many places throughout the guidebook:

- HPT – High Peak Trail
- TT – Tissington Trail
- TPT – Transpennine Trail
- MaT – Manifold Trail
- MoT – Monsal Trail
- MW – Middlewood Way
- Tour de Peak District – this has been shortened in many places to TdPD.

'Towards' or 'To' a Place – where a signpost or map direction takes the rider towards (but not into) a place, it is mentioned as, for example 'towards Longnor'. Where the signpost or map direction actually leads to the place mentioned, it is written as, for example, 'to Longnor'.

Key waypoints

Place names are written in bold in the descriptions if they are identifiable on the route maps provided and are close to the route, giving you an 'at a glance' checklist of key waypoints on the route.

'Bend', 'bear', 'turn', 'sharp' and 'dog-leg'

Generally 'bend' has been used to describe what the road does rather than indicating a junction; 'bear' and 'turn' usually indicate junctions, with 'bear' being a gentler (or oblique) turn than 'turn' or 'sharp turn', which can sometimes be nearly 180°. 'Dog-leg' is used to describe a turn one way closely followed by the opposite, to end up on roughly the original course.

View over Peak District hills at dusk, near Hathersage

ROUTE 1

CHESTERFIELD LOOP VIA TRANSPENNINE TRAIL

Distance	18km
Total ascent/descent	190m
Grade	Easy
Surface	25% road, 65% trail, 10% off-road
Start/finish	Chesterfield Railway Station SK 388 714. Alternative start at Poolsbrook Country Park SK 435 737, useful if combining with Route 6 for a 48km route
Parking	Long stay pay and display car park at the railway station, currently £4 a day after 10am, and various other options nearby. At Poolsbrook height restriction of 2m applies, but some other spaces on nearby roadside verge
Cycle hire	No hire available in Chesterfield, nearest is Hassop Station (1km north of Bakewell)
Road bikes?	Not recommended

A gentle introduction to cycling in the Peak District and Derbyshire, mostly using the TransPennine Trail (TPT) and canal-side trails with just a few harder sections.

Exit Chesterfield railway station and car park rightwards down the road, following blue TPT signs for Staveley via Bridleway Route. Pass through a traffic-light-controlled bridge (ignoring TPT via Canal turning) then rise up to Tapton Park Golf Course entrance on R67/TPT.

Turn left up the golf course driveway following TPT (Brimington Common) signs. Follow the one-way system past the golf course club house and overflow parking onto a dirt vehicle track, found at the far left corner of the car park. Descend this and bend right to a junction. Fork right then bend left onto a shady stony lane, shielded from the fairways by trees. Rise moderately steeply up this, and close to the top beware of golfers teeing off across the trail, followed by a path crossing. Immediately after this, reach a narrow country lane.

Turn left on this and descend gently for 500m. As the lane emerges into housing turn right onto Pettyclose Lane, and 100m later right again onto Balmoak Lane. Descend to a sharp turn right just before a gateway by a dam, then after roughly 300m take a dirt path left through a gate (easy to miss). This uphill is narrow and steep; a sharp bend right signals significant easing of the gradient before a wooden gate through to a vehicle track.

Turn right onto this towards

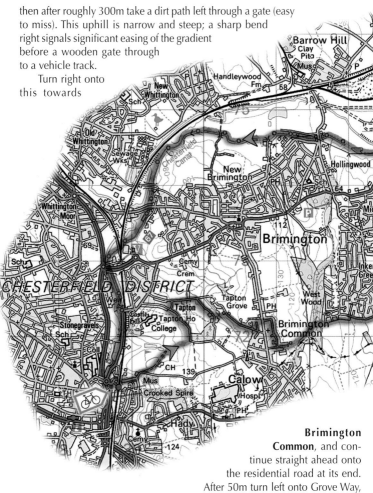

Brimington Common, and continue straight ahead onto the residential road at its end. After 50m turn left onto Grove Way, and turn right at its end onto Recreation Road. Dog-leg right then left across a more major road onto Brooke Drive. This bends right then descends gently for 400m to a T-junction at its end. Turn left towards Pools Brook, and continue straight ahead at the end through A-bars onto a dirt/stone bridleway.

ROUTE 1 CHESTERFIELD LOOP VIA TRANSPENNINE TRAIL

Descend a fairly narrow section of stony track to reach 700m of a lovely wide shady dirt track through sycamore woodland. Continue gently descending, initially beside a small stream. Ignore a narrow fork right, to reach a small concrete bridge over a larger stream. Go slowly on the descent: it could be difficult in wet conditions.

Now rise up quite steeply on the far side of the bridge, following the main trail straight ahead and avoiding side turns to reach two wooden sculptures by Andrew Frost. Continue gently uphill to exit **West Wood** through A-bars. Descend a narrow fenced stony track to reach a residential road. Turn right onto this road and briefly uphill past Blue Bell Close. The road ahead bends left and descends for 600m until reaching a bend left beneath power lines.

Bear right through A-bars onto the TPT and turn left along this, running roughly parallel to the road you've just turned off. Continue straight ahead at the junction for Inkersall Green. Continue for 1.8km, past a school, to pass a turning right to **Poolsbrook Country Park** (toilets and café – summer only Wed–Sun, 10am–4pm).

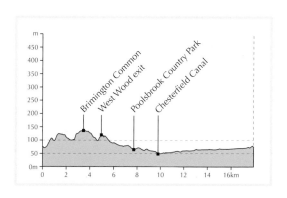

If starting from Poolsbrook Country Park car park, look for a track leading uphill from the visitor centre. This heads past the caravan site to reach the TPT. Turn right along the trail.

Continue along the TPT for 1km past the Inkersall Road car park turning and reach a toucan crossing over a wide road. The next section has numerous A-bars to go through. Cross the road and continue parallel to the road under a bridge before bearing away to the right. At a merging of trails bear left and soon reach a three-way junction of trails. Turn left following TPT (Chesterfield via Canal Loop) and descend gently, first paralleling the current railway line on the right, then coming alongside the newly excavated channel for the canal extension.

One of the two large woodcarved statues at the top of the hill in West Wood

This section of the route currently has a **temporary surface** that may be difficult in wet conditions, and may be temporarily closed during future works to extend the Chesterfield Canal. Check **www.transpenninetrail.org.uk**.

Continue straight ahead under the B6053 road bridge for 1km to reach the end of the **Chesterfield Canal** and start of the canalside Cuckoo Trail. Continue along this trail for 8km to **Chesterfield** town centre. In a couple of places the trail divides into cyclists' and walkers' sections: keep to the cyclists' section, and take care when going underneath bridges, as it's often difficult to see oncoming pedestrians/cyclists. Beware of anglers' rods on the banks of the canal.

Baby ducklings and **dragonflies** are a common sight on this trail in early summer, and sometimes **pied wagtails** can be seen in branches above the canal.

Key waypoints along the canal include Hollingwood Lock and road crossing (A-bars, 2.6km) and Dixon's Lock (3.5km). Less than a kilometre after this, you come to a shady, reed-lined bend just before the red brick bridge of Bilby Lane (4.1km).

A little further on, after Bluebank Lock (4.5km) you are directed right along the Bluebank Loop trail (wider and faster than the canal towpath, but much less scenic). This loop briefly touches the towpath again at Wheeldon Mill Lock (5.7km) and ends with a short steep ascent (dismount) back to the towpath just before Brimington Road North bridge and small car park (6km).

Immediately beyond this is flagstone-lined **Brimington Wharf**. After two railway bridges reach an overbridge at Tapton Lock Visitor Centre (7km or, as the sign says, 2400 km from Istanbul!) tackle a short steep climb (be ready to dismount) followed by a short tunnel. Next comes Tapton Mill Bridge, a small brick footbridge (7.6km), and immediately after this you take a left fork up the bank towards Chesterfield station

Reach the end of this track at a major road; turn right onto the on-road cycle lane (R67). After 900m a short rise leads to a roundabout by The Chesterfield Hotel, and left again onto Station Road – all on an on-road cycle lane. Turn right into Chesterfield Railway station, or if continuing to Poolsbrook, carry on straight ahead downhill, following the instructions from the start.

Three-way junction where the TPT meets the Chesterfield Canal route

ROUTE 2

CARSINGTON RESERVOIR LOOP	
Distance	13km
Total ascent/descent	250m
Grade	Easy
Surface	55% road, 41% trail, 4% off-road
Start/Finish	Carsington Water Visitor Centre SK 240 516
Parking	The main car park (pay and display) at the Visitor Centre is operated by Severn Trent Water. The car park gates are sometimes locked in the evening. 2010 rates were £2.50 (4 hours), £4 all day
Cycle hire	Available at the start of the route from the Watersports and Bike Hire building close to the main Visitor Centre
Road bikes?	Reasonable if detour taken at SK 256 501

There is a traffic free trail making a complete circuit of Carsington Water reservoir; this route makes an interesting variation by including some pleasant country lanes.

When following the lakeside circuit, make sure to follow the blue (cycle route) waymarkers, not the red footpath markers. Beware of hazards, which may include steep descents, sharp and blind bends, other trail users on the 'wrong' side, and skidding on the gravel surface. Murphy's law indicates that these hazards will arise together rather than singly!

From the Visitor Centre car park, head left (facing the reservoir) and past the cycle hire and watersports centre towards Sheepwash, following signs marked north. (Confusingly, the arrow circles the wrong way round, but north is the right direction). Bend right where the car park ends to join R54A, towards the wildlife centre.

The path forks twice by the wildlife centre; stay on the wider path leftwards each time, heading towards Bombing Tower. The track forks in several places from the footpath. Usually the left fork is the cycle path, but it's always clearly marked. Descend round a steep sharp bend to cross a small bridge at the head of an inlet to the reservoir. The track continues, bending left to regain the edge (and views) of the reservoir.

The cycle track bends left to start the detour round a second inlet. The uphill from the inlet crossing is steep, but mercifully short, although there are

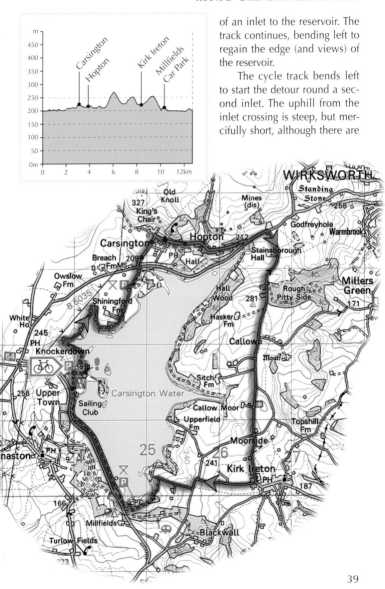

39

a couple of shallow speed bumps to make things a little tougher. Rejoining the reservoir edge again, the track then bends left and briefly loses the reservoir view behind a stand of trees, before a turning right. Detour right here to stop at the Lane End bird hide, otherwise continue on a tarmac track (access for **Shiningford Farm**) past the 'Bombing Tower' towards Sheepwash.

At the end of the track, leave the reservoir circuit trail by bearing left onto the access road to Sheepwash Car Park to reach a road (B5035). Cross this with a dog-leg left then right, and continue ahead on a lane for 400m to Carsington village. Ignore a side-turn right near the brow of the hill as you enter **Carsington** village, and continue downhill to a junction on a sharp bend right.

Follow the main road round to the right, ignoring a further side-turn right and continue past the Miner's Arms PH, and **Hopton Hall** (gardens open some week-days in July/August), with some unusually rounded walls on your right. Continue downhill and round the bend right into **Hopton** village. Ignore a side-road left (where R54A heads uphill) and also a wooden Carsington circuit signpost to the right at the end of the village. Continue straight ahead to reach B5035 again.

Turn left towards Wirksworth, and take care on this short stretch of road which can be busy and fast. In roughly 400m turn right onto a single track lane leading to Callow and Kirk Ireton. About 400m later the road bends gen-tly right, and begins 600m of ascent up the side of Rough Pitty Side (marked

On the road from Hopton to Kirk Ireton

as Soldiers Knoll on some maps). This rises steeply for the first 200-250m after which it eases off to a more gentle gradient. Continue along this lane, with a descent, sometimes slippery, to pass a side-road left for **Callow**, at about 1.7km from the B road.

Continue downhill on the lane ahead, usually now enjoying much drier tarmac, passing a farmer's track to the right (**Sitch Farm**), and a side turn left. The lane then rises briefly but steeply uphill, easing off shortly before a cross-roads with Blind Lane.

Cross over this, and enjoy the downhill to **Kirk Ireton** village, roughly 700m ahead. Continue past a cul-de-sac left, and where Moor Lane becomes Town End, turn right into Gorsey Lane heading towards Hulland. Continue gently up this narrow country lane to reach a T-junction at the road end.

Turn left onto Broom Lane, and very shortly after, reach a side-turn right into Hays Lane. Descend this narrow dead-end road, being careful of horses, potholes and gravel.

> **Alternatively for road-bikes**, continue down the road for a further 1.2km, then turn right onto the main road at a T-junction. Continue along this for roughly 900m and turn right into Millfields Car Park. Turn left before the teeth in the road.

After roughly 250m, just past Riddings Farm, the tarmac mostly ends to be replaced by stones and mud. Continue carefully downhill for a similar distance, to reach a gate across the track ahead.

Pass through a gap beside the gate, and immediately turn left, back onto the reservoir circuit trail, signposted towards Millfields viewing area and visitor centre. This descends gently at first on a well-maintained trail, then more steeply on a concrete path to cross a stream by two junctions. Continue ahead and across the stream at the first and then left and uphill at the second.

Shortly after a set of steps descending to the right, take a sharp right turn towards the visitor centre. Go downhill for 30m through woodland, to then turn left onto a tarmac car park road at the bottom.

Continue straight ahead to exit **Millfields** car park over a very awkward set of teeth in the road. Just 20m later turn sharp right across the road and make a short, steep descent to turn sharp left again onto the ongoing cycle track. Bend right along a tree-lined path to reach a wide cobbled cycle path. This passes a memorial and ends at a circular viewing area near the dam wall.

Head left for a quarter of the way round the viewing area, to gain a short link track. Turn right to continue along the flat and easy cycle track along the dam wall.

Cyclist on Carsington Reservoir Dam Wall

This section can get very busy on sunny summer weekends, but in the quiet of winter and early spring, flocks of **lapwings** (black and white with red beaks) can often be seen on the water.

At the end of the dam wall, pass through an open gateway to reach a junction. Head straight on here, then finally fork right across the access road to the **Sailing Club** back into the Visitor Centre car park.

ROUTE 3

ASHOPTON LOOP VIA DERWENT RESERVOIR

Distance	24km (main route)
Total Ascent/Descent	288m (main route)
Grade	Easy (harder options available)
Surface	55% road, 45% trail
Start/Finish	On-road parking at A57 (Ashopton) SK 191 865 or Fairholmes Car Park SK 172 893 (vehicle use prohibited beyond Fairholmes at weekends and bank holidays)
Parking	Free on road by Ladybower Bridge – can get busy at peak times
Cycle hire	Available from Peak Cycle Hire (Fairholmes)
Road bikes?	Not recommended

This route is good for parties of mixed abilities, with a variety of options to keep most cyclists happy.

Parties with young children may wish to start at the **Fairholmes** Car Park (cycle hire centre) and do a shorter (17km) version of this route; more experienced cyclists with extra energy can extend the route by starting from Bamford Station (Route 5).

↑ map continues on p45

Start from the on-road parking, and follow the pavement-based cyclepath westwards towards Manchester. At the end of the parking area the cyclepath crosses the road to cross the viaduct over Ladybower Reservoir on the right hand side of the road. Beyond the viaduct, turn right up the road for Upper Derwent Dams.

Running alongside the north arm of Ladybower Reservoir, the road gently climbs past the drive for Crookhill Farm before undulating past the first of several

43

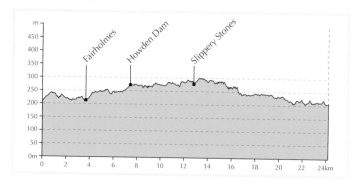

intermediate car parks and Ashopton War Memorial (moved here from its drowned village when the reservoir was built).

After 2.8km go straight ahead at a roundabout at the entrance to **Fairholmes** car park. The road rises up moderately steeply as it passes Derwent Dam, and 1.2km later it bends left to start the 700m detour round **Ouzelden Clough**.

Derwent Reservoir was made famous by **617 Squadron**'s night and altitude precision training flights in preparation for delivering Barnes Wallace's bouncing bomb to the German Ruhr Valley (although no bouncing bombs were actually dropped here).

View along Ladybower Reservoir from Bridge End Car park

Descend gently on this rhododendron-lined road for 350m, then bend right to cross the inlet stream. Rise gently uphill and bend left to resume your northward course. Now look out for an information board on the right.

This marks the site of **Tin Town** – Birchinlee village – a planned settlement by the Water Board for 600–1000 navvies and their families, during the building of the Derwent and Howden Dams in the early 20th Century.

Continue for 1.3km past Tin Town, rising up gently and passing a couple of interesting moss-lined streams on the left as you near the imposing structure of **Howden Dam**. Bend left 250m later to start a 3.5km 'detour' westwards to cross the long River Westend inlet.

Descend gently and bend right to cross an old stone bridge over the long inlet. Follow the road round right and gently uphill for 1.4km.

Bend left to start following the northern arm at a point where a triangular patch of conifers juts out into the reservoir. Ignore a bridleway left and continue on the road ahead for 750m, descending gently overall to the roundabout at the end of the public road. Go through a small wooden gate onto the bridleway to Slippery Stones, surfaced with hard-packed gravel.

↑ map continued from p43   ↓ map continues on p47

45

'Derwent Canteen' – remnants of a 'Tin Town' social building

Descend moderately for 200m bending left to a bridge made of cobbled stone slabs (may be slippery). Continue uphill on a good but steep track through the pine plantation.

The track now undulates briefly for 1km, before descending to a wooden gate, 30m before the bridge at **Slippery Stones**. Descend to cross the bridge and continue upstream on the far side for roughly 100m to reach a junction of paths.

Turn sharp right, following cycle route signs, to take a downstream course. Rise uphill gently on a good solid sandy track below Cold Side for 350m. As the gradient eases you can now see the track gently descending round the reservoir basin for several hundreds of metres ahead.

After roughly 1.5km the track bends gently left before descending on a moderate gradient across the inlet of Howden Clough. Continue along for 1km, to pass **Howden Dam** again, and 500m later cross the bridge over Abbey Brook. Continue along a good smooth track, past a stand of beech trees, and then descend once more (beware of gravel and speed-humps).

If the wind is from the SW (which it typically is) and strong, you may see the **spray** being blown back and upwards from the central spillway of Howden Dam – it's quite a bizarre sight.

Continue along for roughly 1km, to reach a gentle bend left. The view suddenly opens out wide across to Derwent Dam at this point. Continue roughly contouring along for a further 1.2km through very pleasant beech woodland on a good track. Cross an old stone bridge over Hollin Clough and through a small wooden gateway to regain tarmac for the next 700m. At the end of the track join a minor road. (Turn right down the road to end the short route/return hire cycles.)

Bearing left to continue, rise up the tarmac lane, and as you pass Old House Farm look right to see an aqueduct stretching across the reservoir, which looks somewhat out of place. The trail now has two short but steep descents over the next 1.1km. Keep your speed down if it's busy, and look left by the first to see a rare example of hedge-laying. The second descent leads to a bridge over **Mill Brook**, which was once the power supply for an ancient corn mill.

The surface now reverts to well compacted dirt-gravel. Continue gently uphill for 400m and through a small wooden gate as the western-most of the two Ladybower bridges comes into view, ignoring the footpath and side-track left.

Continue gently uphill, before descending on a rougher surface to go through another wooden gate after 650m.

Bend right across the bridge over the inlet stream and the track now undulates for 1.6km, rising slightly overall. As the first gradient eases ignore a rutted vehicle track heading left and continue uphill over slightly rough ground.

Approaching the viaduct again, reach a wooden gate leading onto a tarmac lane at a sharp bend. Take the downhill fork to the A57. Turn right very briefly to cross A57, then turn left onto the cyclepath on the far pavement to return to your start point, or to rejoin Route 5.

↓ map continued from p45

ROUTE 4

MIDDLEWOOD LOOP VIA LYME PARK

Distance	20km
Total ascent/descent	335m
Grade	Easy
Surface	63% road, 28% trail, 9% off-road (easy)
Start/finish	Middlewood Station (by rail) SJ 945 848 or Nelson's Pit Visitor Centre (by car) SJ 945 834
Getting to the start (road)	A523 to Poynton, turn onto Park Lane, fork left onto Middlewood Road, then right onto Anson Road. Cross Shrigley Road North and turn left into car park
Parking	Free parking at Nelson's Pit Visitor Centre Car Park, Higher Poynton (height restriction 2.0m – nearby layby parking may be possible for overheight vehicles)
Cycle hire	Nearest available is Peak Tours (Glossop) or Longdendale Valley (Hadfield)
Additional info	It's worth picking up a copy of the Middlewood Way guide from www.macclesfield.gov.uk/pdfs/MidWayGuide.pdf
Road bikes?	May struggle on West Park Gate Trail, otherwise reasonable

This route goes through Lyme Park, and provides an interesting alternative to the standard 'out and back' along the rail trail.

The Middlewood Way is one of the less well known 'rail trails' near the Peak District. It runs from Macclesfield to Marple.

From the station, head uphill from the platform to reach Bridge 19 over the railway. Head south along the Middlewood Way for roughly 1.1km to reach the restored station platforms close to the Nelson's Pit **Visitor Centre** and car park. **From the car park** exit past the height limiting barrier. Cross the road and descend the steps to reach the Middlewood Way by an old station whose platforms now carry the cycle track. Go straight ahead (south).

Continue for 2.2km to reach bridge 12 (the sign is difficult to spot, hidden by branches on the right). Immediately before this bridge, fork right and up some steps following a sign for a tea shop and the Miners' Arms pub. Turn right at the top, away from the bridge and marina, to reach a crossroads at **Wood Lanes**. Turn left onto Wood Lane South, and take this undulating lane which descends to a narrow bridge before rising to a triangular junction.

Bear left up Roundy Lane towards Pott Shrigley; continue for 850m, then bear left at the next junction. Pass Roundy House and over the Middlewood Way.

Although it is possible to continue along the Middlewood Way and exit here, the **stile** is extremely awkward for cyclists.

Continue along for a further 800m, passing over the canal, and entering a very pleasant shady sycamore-lined part of the road. Bear left at the end of the lane and enter **Pott Shrigley** on a wider road.

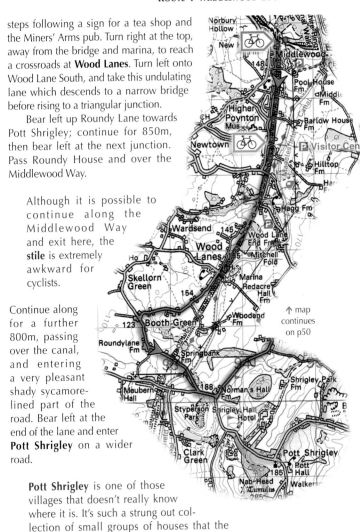

↑ map continues on p50

Pott Shrigley is one of those villages that doesn't really know where it is. It's such a strung out collection of small groups of houses that the entire village spans more than 5km (3 miles), with signs announcing its entrance, then 100m later saying it's still 3 miles away!

Rise up moderately steeply to a junction on a steep bend and turn left into Shrigley Road, past Norman's Hall Farm. Continue for 1.3km, ignoring a bridle-way just before a café and rise steeply up the next bend right past Harrop Brow.

↑ map
continues
on p52

Continue straight ahead past a couple of lovely white-painted cottages and roughly 100m after the steep descent warning sign, look out for Pott Shrigley Methodist Church on the right. Fork right at the church on the tarmac track leading almost parallel to the road (NOT the stone track at right-angles to the road). **Dismount** and walk for the next 150m as this track only has footpath rights, and turn right by West Lodge to enter Lyme Park's **West Parkgate**.

→ map
continued
from p49

Lyme Park is a National Trust property, and was previously owned by the Legh family between the 14th century and 1946. It was extensively redesigned to a style similar to that of an Italian palace in the early 18th century by Venetian architect, Giacomo Leoni.

Cycling is only permitted on the tarmac roads and the main stone tracks, including the West Park track. Cyclists should beware of both pedestrians and vehicular traffic on the grounds. Opening hours of the grounds are 8.00am to 6.00pm daily, sometimes to 8.00pm in summer.

Rise up a stone-cobbled track through shady woodland for 1.2km, ignoring two minor paths joining from the right. You may smell the fresh pungent aroma

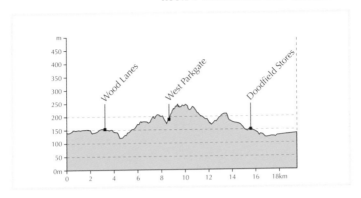

of wild garlic early on, and you soon gain a shallow stream to the right. As the track gets higher, the valley begins to open out, with good displays of bluebells in spring, and some rhododendrons in summer. The stone track ends with a wooden gate into The Knott Car Park.

Go straight ahead through the car park, and follow the tarmac access road over a gentle rise and downhill over a cattle grid to reach the main car park of

Cyclist emerging from tunnel under the A6 on Middlewood Way

Lyme Park, and nearby refreshments (café/kiosk). Rise up 100m beyond the car park and turn left at the T-junction at the top. Descend gently on the estate access road for 2km, past the entrance kiosk and over a cattle grid to reach the main **Parkgate** to reach the A6.

Inexperienced riders may wish to dismount to cross this busy road, otherwise take a dog-leg left then right onto Light Alders Lane. An initially steep hill soon gives way to a gentle rise up this quiet backroad. Turn left at the T-junction at the top and descend on a traffic-calmed road back towards the A6. Just 50m before reaching the main road, turn right onto Beechway, then left at the end onto Thornway.

Descend on this, taking the second right on South Meadway. Continue on this winding residential road for 500m to reach a T-junction at its end. Turn right

↑ map
continued
from p50

Cyclist on MIddlewood Way, before Jackson's Brickworks south of the station

onto another traffic-calmed road and descend for 800m, over the Macclesfield Canal to another T-junction at the end of Andrew Lane.

Turn right on this more major road, which gently rises and then falls to a junction just before **Doodfield** Stores. Turn left here into Torkington Lane, which makes several sharp bends before crossing the Middlewood Way. It's not possible to access the trail from this bridge, instead follow the road parallel to the trail for another 250m, to reach an access to the trail between two houses where the road next bends sharply right.

Turn right along the trail to head south and back to either **Middlewood** rail station (2.3km) or Nelson's Pit (Visitor Centre) car park (3.4km) at **Higher Poynton**.

ROUTE 5

BAMFORD LOOP VIA LADYBOWER

Distance	18km (not counting parts of route described in Route 3)
Total ascent/descent	290m (not counting parts of route described in Route 3)
Grade	Moderate
Surface	54% road, 14% trail, 32% off-road
Start/finish	Bamford Railway Station Car Park SK 207 825
Cycle hire	Available from Peak Cycle Hire (Fairholmes)
Road bikes?	Not recommended

This route is a good extension for the faster more experienced cyclists in parties of mixed abilities doing Route 3, although it uses the busy A57 for 3km between Great Wood and the Derwent Access Road.

Slower, less experienced parties may wish to do Route 3, and really keen MTBers may be interested in a tough off-road detour via Crookhill Farm onto the ridge-line, right at Woodcock Coppice and descending via a steep and very rough track towards Ouzelden Clough, but that is not a route for the off-road novice! This route is best done in dry conditions.

Ladybower Reservoir Dam Wall

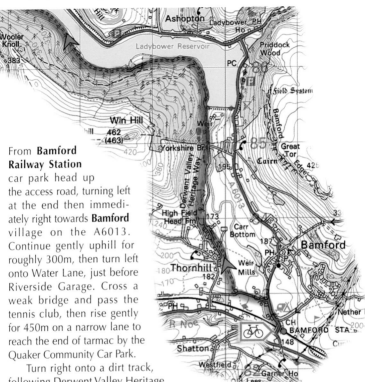

From **Bamford Railway Station** car park head up the access road, turning left at the end then immediately right towards **Bamford** village on the A6013. Continue gently uphill for roughly 300m, then turn left onto Water Lane, just before Riverside Garage. Cross a weak bridge and pass the tennis club, then rise gently for 450m on a narrow lane to reach the end of tarmac by the Quaker Community Car Park.

Turn right onto a dirt track, following Derwent Valley Heritage Way signs to **Yorkshire Bridge** on a new bridleway (Thornhill Trail). Continue straight ahead up this former railway line for 1.5km to reach a country lane, passing four gates and two vehicle crossings on the way. The final 10m is a very sharp, narrow and moderately steep bend left, which may be best to walk down.

Cross over the country lane and follow the continuation of the Thornhill Trail for roughly 1.25km, passing an access control and gate near the start. Pass through a gate after 1km, and finally reach a tarmac road. Turn left and uphill on this concessionary bridleway, the gradient eases some 300m later as you pass a footpath joining across the **Ladybower Reservoir** dam wall.

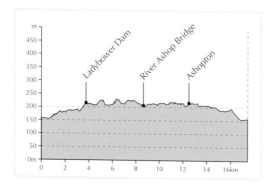

Continue ahead on the concessionary bridleway along the western arm of the reservoir for roughly 6km to reach the A57, staying on the main track throughout, and being aware of both sheep and forestry/anglers vehicles on the track, and often very muddy patches near to logpiles.

The spillway '**plughole**' can be very impressive when the reservoir is very full!

Along the way, the tarmac disappears roughly 300m from the dam wall, by a forestry loading area. The track now dips, rises then dips once more over a short rougher section.

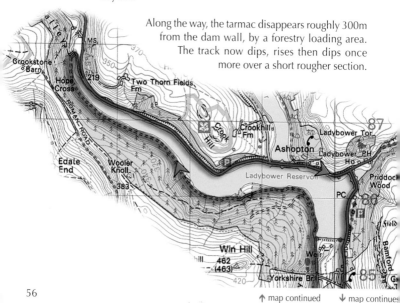

56

↑ map continued from p55   ↓ map continues on p58

Continue along a deteriorating stone track to reach a pair of wooden gateposts roughly 1.5km from the dam wall.

Rise briefly, on a slightly rough surface, then descend for 400m on a reasonable (if often muddy) surface to the reservoir edge, where views of the western arm of Ladybower Reservoir now begin to open out. Pass a leat and small stream (often dry) on the left and rise up a somewhat cobbled section to cross a second larger stream. Rise gently up another roughly cobbled section to gain a bit of height over the reservoir (roughly 3km from dam wall).

Descend once more and as you rise up the far side, beware of another short logpile area. Continue gently uphill, now on a drier track, passing a steep bridleway on the left at the next summit, with fine views over the western end of the reservoir (roughly 4.5km from dam wall).

Descend once again past a couple of logpile areas as the reservoir begins to narrow towards its western end, reaching a small junction with a track leading uphill to Hagg Farm. Fork right and over a bridge crossing the River Ashop, then through a small wooden gate to the side of the locked metal gates.

Rise gently uphill and through a wooden gate, just before passing the green forestry commission metal barrier. Continue on tarmac to the A57, then turn right to follow this busy, fast and undulating road for 3km to **Ashopton**, passing the tempting mobile Ladybower café on the way (open roughly 7.45am to 2.30pm, later on summer weekends).

Ladybower Reservoir – North Arm bridge in the distance

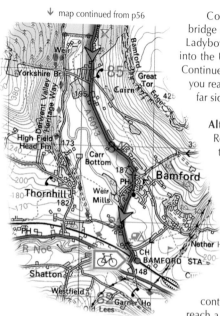

↓ map continued from p56

Continue on to reach the bridge over the northern arm of the Ladybower Reservoir, and turn left into the Upper Derwent access road. Continue along on Route 3 here until you reach the A57 once more on the far side of the bridge.

Alternatively if not doing Route 3 as well, cut across the bridge– it's usually best to ignore the cycle track at first, then make use of it once it's crossed to the right-hand side of the road at the far end of the bridge.

Rejoining the route on the far side of the bridge, continue along the cycle path to reach a traffic-light-controlled junction by the bridge over the eastern arm of the Reservoir. Turn right on the cycle path, and once past Heatherdene Car Park, take any good (early) opportunity to cross onto the road between there and 50m before the end of Ladybower Reservoir (where cyclists are required to dismount, effectively marking the end of the cyclepath beside the road.)

Continue on the A6013 past the Yorkshire Bridge Inn, and descend through **Bamford** Village to reach the station access road some 3.5km from the Ladybower dam wall. Fork left onto this to return to the station car park.

ROUTE 6

ASHBOURNE LOOP VIA HOGNASTON

Distance	32km
Total ascent/descent	560m
Grade	Moderate
Surface	78% road, 22% trail
Start/finish	NW edge of Ashbourne, Tissington Trail Car Park (Mapleton Lane) SK 176 469
Getting to the start	Initially follow signs for A515 Buxton and DoveDale from town centre. Good signposting for the Tissington Trail appears on A515 (North) with a left turn immediately after the market square
Parking	The car park is owned by Peak District National Park, and is pay and display between 10am and 6pm every day; 2010 rates were £2.50 for 4 hours, £3.50 all day
Cycle hire	Available at the start of the route from Peak Cycle Hire
Road bikes?	Reasonable

Mostly undulating and quiet country lanes, with an easy last section on the Tissington Trail (TT).

Cyclist on R68 through Ashbourne

From Mapleton Lane Car Park, head southwards on the cycle track through the tunnel to reach a gate leading into a car park.

The next section runs along R68 and is well signed within Ashbourne's residential areas. Continue ahead through the car park, passing the leisure centre on your left. Turn right at the T-junction at the end of the road, and after 500m (shortly before a roundabout) turn left into an unnamed residential road (Lodge Road). At its end, after 200m, turn left, then after 100m turn right onto a tarmac cyclepath at the start of Highfield Road. After only a further 30m, turn left up a path which rises for 500m, passing between houses and fields, to arrive at the dead end of a cul-de-sac (Forshaw Close). Continue ahead along here, turn right at its end along Duncombe Drive, and at the next T-junction turn left. In a further 100m you reach a roundabout outside a primary school.

Turn right at the roundabout and continue out of Ashbourne on a country lane. It's worth keeping your nerve as much as possible on the

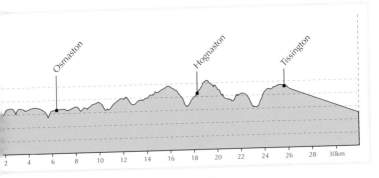

↑ map continues on p63

steep downhill, which passes under the A52 road bridge in a deep dip, to gain some gravity assistance as it rises steeply back up the far side.

Continue past Ashbourne Golf Club and Dobbin Horse Lane on the right to reach a T-junction 2.5km from the roundabout. Turn left, leaving R68 and continue along a plateau–level country lane to **Osmaston**, with a steep and narrow dip after roughly 800m.

Osmaston is a pretty little village with a pleasant duck pond surrounded by thatched cottages as you enter from this direction, and Osmaston Hall is worth a detour to explore the public footpaths in its grounds (on foot of course!) and see the historic and highly photogenic sawmill.

From the duck pond, stay left on the main road, continuing past the Shoulder of Mutton PH, and roughly 400m later reach a junction by the village church. Turn right towards Brailsford to reach the A52. Cross this busy road with care into Ladyhole Lane, and continue past Ladyhole hamlet over a cattle grid, where the lane becomes unfenced through pasture land. Cross a second cattle grid and turn left at the T-junction signposted Moorend to reach the hamlet of **Hole in the Wall**.

Turn right onto Hadley Lane (just 80m before the obvious 'Hole in the Wall'), then after 700m turn left towards Bradley at a T-junction. After a further 200m turn right at a triangle junction towards Mercaston on Yew Tree Lane. Ignore a side-road on the right, and continue to The Knob hamlet, some 1.25km after the triangle junction. Turn left off Pinfold Lane at a second tri-angle junction towards Hulland. Continue along this

gently undulating country lane to reach the A517 in roughly 1.2km. Turn left towards Ashbourne, continue round a sharp bend right, then turn right for Hognaston as the road bends back sharply left. Continue up this road ignoring an unsigned side road left and a staggered cross-roads, to reach a more convention-ally shaped crossroads roughly 1.8km from the A517. Turn left to Hognaston on Turlow Fields Lane; the road descends steeply to cross the Henmore Brook soon after a side road joins from the left, before heading back uphill into **Hognaston** village after roughly 2km.

Keep on the main road through the village, past St Bartholemew's Parish Church and the Red Lion Inn. Continue moderately uphill, ignoring a side road left at the top of the hill. Roughly 150m later the road ends at a T-junction with the B5053, some 1.6km from the start of the village. Turn right towards Wirksworth, and roughly 100m later left towards Bradbourne along an undulating winding lane on R54A. Arriving in **Bradbourne** 2.5km later, turn left at the T-junction, and enjoy roughly 1km of downhill to reach the B5056.

Turn left towards Ashbourne, then after 300m bear right towards a ford, which is avoided by a narrow bridge. The road heads uphill, steeply at first to reach a high, partly unfenced plateau on a narrow country lane with cattle grids. Roughly 2km after the ford you approach **Tissington** village. Almost immediately after passing over an easily missed bridge, turn sharp left to enter the TT car park.

Bear to the right and end of the car park and head back down the TT for roughly 6km to regain the starting point in Ashbourne.

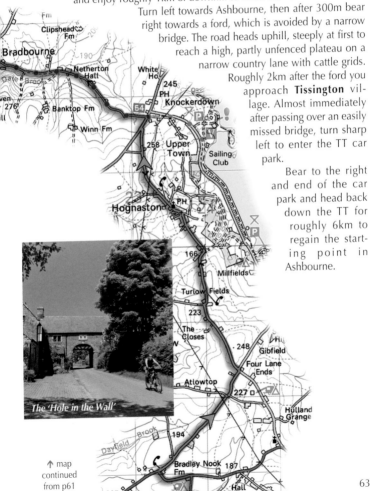

The 'Hole in the Wall'

↑ map continued from p61

63

ROUTE 7

CHESTERFIELD LOOP
VIA HOLYMOORSIDE AND LEASH FEN

Distance	30km
Total ascent/descent	480m
Grade	Moderate
Surface	74% road, 12% trail, 14% off-road
Start/finish	Chesterfield Railway Station SK 388 714
Parking	Long stay pay and display car park at the railway station, currently £4.00 per day after 10am: various other options nearby
Cycle hire	Nearest at Hassop Station (near Bakewell) some 17km west (as the crow flies)
Road bikes?	Detour to avoid Linacre Woods

Out past some urban art and Walton Dam, some pleasant high moorland, and returning via Linacre Woods.

Exit Chesterfield Railway station via the access road turning left onto the on-road cycle lane. Stay on this to go left past the Chesterfield Hotel, then cross the A61 slipway with care. Dismount briefly to cross a footbridge over the A61 dual carriageway.

Continue past a bar on the right and go straight ahead onto Station Road. Consider a detour to see the Crooked Spire, or continue past the Derbyshire Times office to the end of the road. Turn right at the cobbled junction opposite the Spa Lane Vaults PH. Turn left onto the busy main road, over a pedestrian crossing, and make an awkward right turn at the bottom of the hill into Beetwell Street. Turn right to continue straight ahead by Vicar Lane Car Park, and go past the coach terminus. Continue for 500m along this road, to reach a pedestrian crossing at the top of a slight rise, with the Town Hall imposing on your right.

Turn left here to follow a cycleway through an arch in a glass fronted building. Dismount to cross the A619 dual carriageway by a footbridge, and make a sharp right turn half way down the descent ramp before remounting at a cycle path which also passes under the bridge.

Admire the amazing urban art under the bridge, and turn left along the cycle path, which leads to a car park after 200m. Follow the cycle lane across miniature railway tracks and out to a road through some grand gates.

Cross the road via the toucan crossing and continue along Dock Walk past Travis Perkins and later the Unicorn Tavern PH. Continue for 400m until you reach a junction on a bend. Turn right to continue straight ahead along Goytside Road for 450m, through an area rich in industrial heritage, past the Robinson Packaging works to reach the blue gates of an old factory. Continue straight ahead through barriers onto a short cycle path running through this derelict area.

Note Redevelopment may change the appearance of this part of the route in the future.

The cycle path ends at the back of Morrisons. Turn left onto Walgrove Road and almost immediately right onto Bobbin Mill Lane. Bend left onto a side-road just before the Morrisons petrol station. Turn left at the end onto a cycle lane beside a major road and 70m later turn right across the toucan crossing onto a cycle track towards Somersall.

The track soon passes Walton Dam and continues alongside the River Hipper through a pleasant shady woodland for roughly 600m. Turn left over a small stone

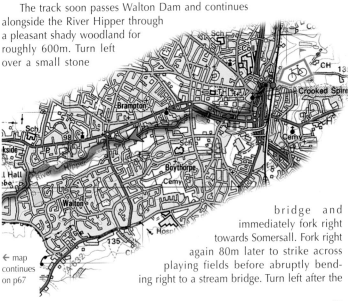

bridge and immediately fork right towards Somersall. Fork right again 80m later to strike across playing fields before abruptly bending right to a stream bridge. Turn left after the

← map continues on p67

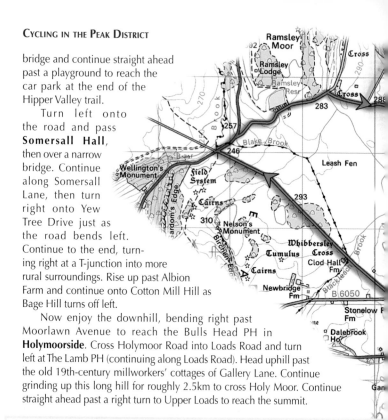

bridge and continue straight ahead past a playground to reach the car park at the end of the Hipper Valley trail.

Turn left onto the road and pass **Somersall Hall**, then over a narrow bridge. Continue along Somersall Lane, then turn right onto Yew Tree Drive just as the road bends left. Continue to the end, turning right at a T-junction into more rural surroundings. Rise up past Albion Farm and continue onto Cotton Mill Hill as Bage Hill turns off left.

Now enjoy the downhill, bending right past Moorlawn Avenue to reach the Bulls Head PH in **Holymoorside**. Cross Holymoor Road into Loads Road and turn left at The Lamb PH (continuing along Loads Road). Head uphill past the old 19th-century millworkers' cottages of Gallery Lane. Continue grinding up this long hill for roughly 2.5km to cross Holy Moor. Continue straight ahead past a right turn to Upper Loads to reach the summit.

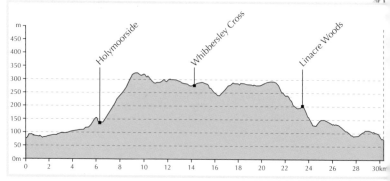

Turn right towards Eastmoor on Syda Lane, and look back to see how much you've climbed! Follow this bending and undulating road for 2.5km, avoiding all right turns and enjoying the view, until you reach a crossing of the A619 on an awkward bend near Eastmoor. Cross straight over the main road towards Cutthorpe.

Continue straight ahead for 650m to a skewed cross-roads with a wider road. Turn left towards Baslow and 600m later, as this road bends left, bear right towards Curbar, then 100m later cross the B6050. Continue straight ahead for 3km, passing Clod Hall Farm.

Whibbersley Cross, a medieval waymarker marking one of the boundaries of the treacherous Leash Fen, is barely visible from the road, and is on the right, not left as marked on OS maps. Leash Fen is thought to have once been a prosperous medieval market town, larger than Chesterfield, which suddenly sank one day into the deep bog. Another strange old distance marker, looking more like a grave stone, is in the drystone wall on the left 600m after Clod Hill Farm.

At a bend left, descend moderately to the A621. Turn right towards Sheffield on this busy road, and 350m later fork right towards Millthorpe and

→ map continues on p 68

← map continued from p65

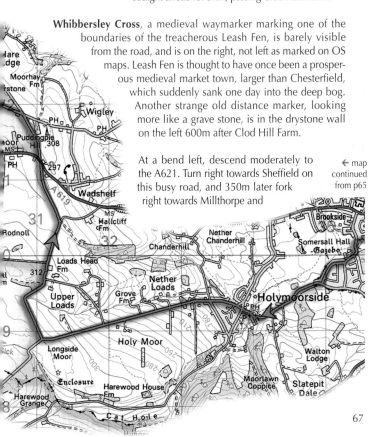

Shillito Woods for 1.5km. Turn right towards Barlow. Turn right towards Baslow after 1.1km and descend gently on a winding lane for 500m. Next fork left and continue along this plateau-level road for 1.2km to reach the B6050 again. Bear left on the B road and enjoy a fantastic 2km descent past The Gate PH.

About 1km and several bends after the pub, take a right turn onto the access road for **Linacre Reservoirs**. This narrow tarmac road first gently climbs, and then turns to descend past car parks (often with ice cream van).

Road cyclists may prefer to continue on the B6050 then B6051 into Chesterfield.

Continue straight ahead past the toilet building, where the track becomes a pleasant dirt bridleway through woodland (poor surface when wet). Ignore a right turn at a junction by a bridge after 350m; the track then runs parallel to a small stream for a short while. The track now rises moderately for 400m. Pass a house (right) and 40m later continue straight ahead for 700m at a junction by a field corner. The tarmac drive to Hadfield Barns signals (almost) the end of the track, with a very short descent over somewhat rougher terrain to meet the Chesterfield–Old Brampton road.

Turn left and descend for roughly 3.2km towards **Chesterfield** centre, going straight over the round-about by The Woodside PH on Ashgate Road. Pass The Crispin PH, and rise up gently after

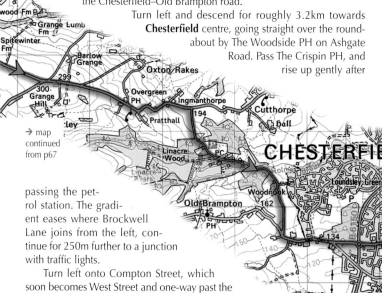

passing the petrol station. The gradient eases where Brockwell Lane joins from the left, continue for 250m further to a junction with traffic lights.

Turn left onto Compton Street, which soon becomes West Street and one-way past the

Summer blossom in the foreground over Leash Fen

council offices. Turn right at the end into Cross Street (still one-way). Continue for 250m past the primary school and baptist church, before turning left onto Queen Street.

Continue along this (two-way now) and turn right at the end by the Chesterfield Arms. Continue past Holy Trinity Church (where George Stephenson is buried) and turn slightly right towards the town centre over a mini roundabout, heading directly towards the Crooked Spire.

Continue over a pedestrian crossing to a larger roundabout. Take the first left off the roundabout by The Old Post Restaurant onto Durrant Road towards the station. Descend past a turn to the Magistrates Court and bend right, crossing the A61 on a bridge. Continue straight ahead over a roundabout, following signs for the railway station. Take the next left in roughly 80m and the station is just on the right.

ROUTE 8

TISSINGTON LOOP VIA ELTON

Distance	47km
Total ascent/descent	990m
Grade	Moderate
Surface	54% road, 35% trail, 11% off-road
Start/finish	TT Car Park on the south-east edge of Tissington Village SK 177 521
Parking	The car park is operated by Peak District National Park, and is pay and display between 10am and 6pm every day: 2010 rates were £2.50 for 4 hours, £3.50 all day
Cycle hire	Available in Ashbourne (roughly 8km south on the TT) from Peak Cycle Hire
Road bikes?	Reasonable with detours

Mostly undulating and quiet country lanes, with some adventurous (avoidable) off-road, and an easy last section on the Tissington Trail.

The High Peak Trail (HPT) and Tissington Trail (TT) are not marked as such on some maps. Instead they both are marked as Pennine Bridleway (PBW). HPT runs roughly south-east from Parsley Hay to Cromford, TT runs roughly south from Parsley Hay to Ashbourne.

Ignoring the TT for now, leave the car park via the access road. Turn sharp right onto Darfield Lane, and cross the railway bridge on R54A. The road goes over three cattle grids near Broadbent Farm, descending increasingly steeply after the second and third, to reach the B5056 at a ford in roughly 2.5km. Don't take the second descent too quickly, it gets narrow and twisty at the bottom, and oncoming cars have a blind summit. Avoid the **ford** via a narrow bridge (left).

Just beyond the ford, a new extension to R54A forks right across the main road – use this if you like lots of gates to miss out a short section of road! Otherwise, cross the cattle grid, turn left and take the next right onto a country lane towards Bradbourne.

Head uphill for 1km into **Bradbourne** village, ignoring a fork right to Carsington where R54A leaves your route. Continue uphill on the country lane, the gradient easing past the recently renovated Bryn Hall Farm.

Ignore a side-turn left to Ballidon and descend gently into **Brassington** village. Continue past Ye Olde Gate PH and the church to emerge outside the Miners Arms PH. Continue ahead (left) along Maddock Lane to reach the main road through the village.

At the end of this lane, turn left onto Dale End. Head uphill out of the village, and in roughly 300m turn right towards Wirksworth. The road briefly rises before undulating gently

← map continues on p73

past Harboro Rocks – a fascinating series of small limestone outcrops popular with novice climbers. The road now runs parallel to HPT for 2km, passing two stone processing works and descending to a crossroads in the bottom of a long dip in the road.

Turn left under a high stone arch towards Grangemill, and enjoy a steepening 1.9km descent beside **Hopton Wood**.

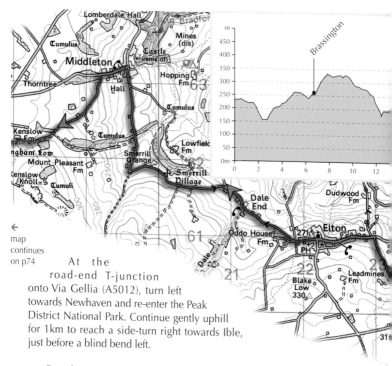

←
map
continues
on p74

At the road-end T-junction onto Via Gellia (A5012), turn left towards Newhaven and re-enter the Peak District National Park. Continue gently uphill for 1km to reach a side-turn right towards Ible, just before a blind bend left.

From late spring onwards a pleasant but pervasive smell of **wild garlic** permeates the air throughout Via Gellia.

Turn right up this narrow country lane and rise up fairly steeply past the remnants of some old works buildings, then round a hairpin. At a second hairpin, bend left and uphill on the often muddy road, ignoring two side-tracks off to the right. The gradient eases again as you enter **Ible** village some 300m later.

After roughly 500m and as the houses end, turn right onto a narrow and unsigned tarmac lane and then head moderately steeply uphill to reach a desolate junction near the crest of the ridge (SK 253 578) where a more major road joins from the left. Carry straight on, soon losing the tarmac, for roughly 700m to reach a second junction with another tarmac road (SK 255 584). Turn left, rising gently across **Bonsall Moor** on a gated road, then descending gently to a T-junction in roughly 1.1km.

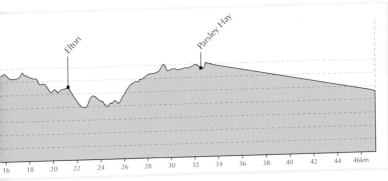

Turn left towards Bakewell, and descend gently past a few derelict barns to the B5056. Turn right towards Bakewell, then soon afterwards turn left onto a side-road. Cross a further junction 100m later to gain a restricted byway opposite (Limestone Way).

If you wish **to avoid the rough section** ahead, turn left here, and then take all right turns to bring you to Elton Church to rejoin the route.

The first part of this byway has a narrow rocky descent, but then much improves after passing over a farm track, to reach a tarmac road opposite Dudwood Lane.

Turn left and head into **Elton**. Continue through the village on the main road past the church, just opposite which (up a side-road) was once the Elton tea shop, renowned among local cyclists for its Aga cooking and home-made cakes but now sadly closed.

Continue straight ahead to exit the village on the road west, descending towards Gratton. A 1km-long gentle descent on a

↑ map continued from p71

73

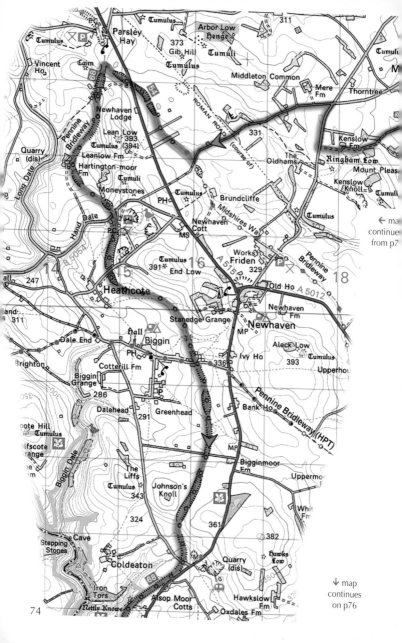

Tumulus
311
Parsley
Hay
P
Vincent
Ho
Cairn
Arbor Low
Henge
373
Gib Hill
Cumuli
Tumulus
Middleton Common
Mere
Fm
Thorntree
Newhaven
Lodge
Lean Low
393
(394)
Leanlow Fm
Hartington-moor
Fm
Moneystones
Quarry
(dis)
Long Dale
Hand Dale
Kenslow
Fm
331
(course of)
The
Oldhams
Ringham Low
Mount Pleas
Kenslow
Knoll
Tumuli
Tumulus
PH
Tumulus
PC
Tumulus
Brundcliffe
Midshires Way
Newhaven
Cott
MS
Tumulus
Cumulus
Works
Friden
End Low
329
A 515
Old Ho
A 5012
Pennine
Bridleway
Newhaven
Fm
Newhaven
14
15
16
391
247
Tumulus
Heathcote
Stanedge Grange
MP
Newhaven
18
Dale End
Hall
Biggin
Ivy Ho
Aleck Low
393
Tumulus
Upperhou
Brighton
311
PH
Cotterill Fm
336
Biggin
Grange
286
P
Pennine Bridleway (HPT)
Bank Ho
Dalehead
291
Greenhead
cote Hill
Tumulus
lifscote
range
Biggin Dale
The
Liffs
Tumulus
343
Johnson's
Knoll
324
MP
Bigginmoor
Fm
Uppermo
361
382
Whit
Fm
Cave
Stepping
Stones
MP
Quarry
(dis)
Hawks
Low
Coldeaton
Iron
Tors
Nettly Knowe
Alsop Moor
Cotts
Oxdales Fm
Hawkslow
Fm

74

← map
continue
from p7

↓ map
continues
on p76

Looking back along Whitfield Lane

narrow lane passes Dale End Farm; fork left and uphill by 'The Cheese Factory' roughly 250m later.

Continue uphill past an intriguing two-faced stone sculpture, past Smerrill Grange Farm. The road undulates for 1.3km before descending easily into **Middleton**. Continue past a small village green to reach a wide junction in the centre of the village. Turn left and uphill for roughly 500m out of the village.

As the road starts to enter woodland turn sharp left onto Whitfield Lane, and continue steeply uphill. The tarmac track eventually descends to arrive in front of Little Rookery Farm. In front of the farmhouse, turn right along a narrow tarmac lane, through the first of several gates along the next section. The lane soon arrives at Kenslow Farm, where the trail makes a dog-leg left then right past the muddy farmyard, to exit onto the road through a final gate.

To **avoid** the fairly adventurous **off-road section** next, turn left along this road to the Friden car park, then take HPT north-west towards Parsley Hay. The off-road route rejoins after roughly 650m on HPT.

Otherwise, turn right onto the tarmac road, continue ahead for 600m to a crossroads in a wooded area, and turn left onto a tarmac track towards Mere Farm.

The tarmac remains mostly intact up the initial gentle rise for 700m or so. After this the next 1.4 km holds descents and ascents on a variety of entertaining loose rock, mud and ruts, and rapidly forms a puddle lane in wet conditions.

On a slight rise you reach a junction with the **HPT**. Turn right onto this through a wooden gate. Continue easily for 1.8km towards Parsley Hay, passing through a short tunnel under the A515 on the way. When you reach the junction where the TT joins from your left, turn sharp left (back on yourself) to head back for 16km on this straightforward trail to Tissington car park.

Cyclist coming over Wibben Hill (just east of Tissington)

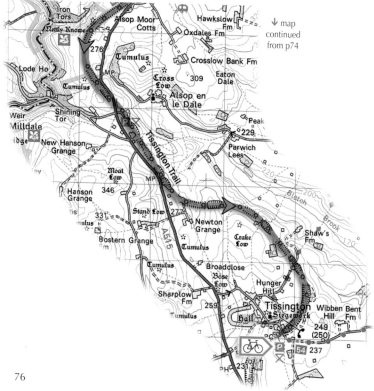

↓ map continued from p74

ROUTE 9

WIRKSWORTH LOOP VIA HARTINGTON

Distance	47km
Total ascent/descent	865m
Grade	Moderate
Surface	51% road, 39% trail, 10% off-road
Start/finish	Middleton Top Car Park SK 276 552
Parking	The car park at Middleton Top is currently on an honesty box system, but is expected to become pay and display in the future
Cycle hire	Available at the start of the route from Middleton Top
Road bikes?	Reasonable with detour avoiding Cardlemere Lane (see below)

Country lanes take you up past an old monastic grange to the picturesque village of Hartington, and easily back down the High Peak Trail (HPT).

The High Peak Trail (HPT) and Tissington Trail (TT) are not marked as such on some maps. Instead they both are marked as Pennine Bridleway (PBW). HPT runs roughly south-east from Parsley Hay to Cromford, TT runs roughly south from Parsley Hay to Ashbourne.

At Middleton Top, descend the tarmac access road to the B5035, and take this right towards Ashbourne for 1.1km, taking care on this winding and busy road. At a crossroads turn right onto a narrow country lane, and begin to grind up a hill towards Brassington.

Despite its beauty this is one of the Peak District's main **quarrying** areas, as is visible from the working and no-longer-used quarries on your right, so keep an eye out for quarry lorries.

At the road's summit, you will see the HPT in the distance running parallel to the road – this is your return route. For now, descend the hill, taking care as roads join from both directions in the dip, and continue up the far side. Continue along this undulating road for 3.2km, with glimpses of Carsington

Reservoir and Harboro Rocks, to reach a T-junction above Brassington, where you will lose virtually all quarry traffic.

Turn left and down the hill into **Brassington**. Just before you enter the village take a small lane on your right, marked 'Unsuitable for motor vehicles', rise up briefly, then begin to drop down Kings Hill. The lane soon forks, turn left to go straight ahead on Jaspers Lane. This lane ends at a T-junction with a postbox opposite. Turn right here, then right again onto the Bradbourne road running past the Miners Arms pub. Continue past Ye Olde Gate Inn pub and, where the road changes name to Well Street, follow it out of the village.

About 200 metres after the last houses, take a right turn signposted to Ballidon, going uphill at first. As you reach

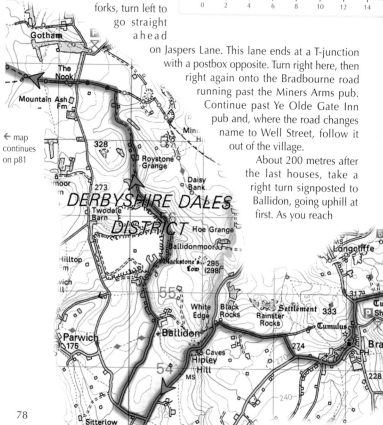

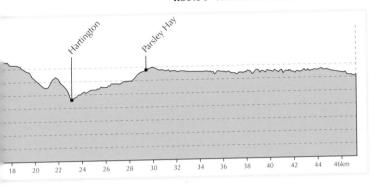

the summit you will see some amazing limestone outcrops ahead – these are **Rainster Rocks.** Bend sharply left to run parallel to the dry wide grassy vale on your right for roughly 1km, before finally dropping down into this vale to reach a junction with the B5056.

Turn left towards Ashbourne (you may briefly meet quarry traffic again, heading towards Ballidon), and drop gently down through a narrow limestone gorge.

The **caves** marked on the OS map are not very visible in this direction, being somewhat hidden by hawthorn bushes.

The road then flattens out and 1.6km after joining the B5056, you reach a turning to the right. Take this towards Ballidon past White Meadow Farm to reach a second turning right. Continue up this country lane

for 1.2km, across another wide grassy vale and pass through the hamlet of **Ballidon**.

The road continues through the hamlet to a quarry. At the quarry entrance you are confronted with a confusing array of options; take the right-most road (which feels wrong but is correct). Continue 300m along this lane past Tarmac's TopBlock driveway, and straight over a cattle grid.

The road (Roystone Lane) now narrows to become a lovely, quiet country lane along a typical limestone dry valley. You will pass through a number of gates, which may be open or closed.

After about 1.3km you pass an unusual grilled-window building on your left. This is an old **19th-century pump house** built to serve the quarries along the railway line that is now the HPT. However, the site has a much older history, being built on the remains of the grange buildings of a former monastic lead-mining and sheep farm from the 12th–14th centuries.

Riding up the Royston Grange track, with hawthorn flowering in background

Shortly after the pump house you rise to pass through the farmyard of **Roystone Grange**, which was built in the 16th century, shortly after the land changed ownership with the Dissolution of the Monasteries. The lane continues to climb gently up the valley, culminating in a T-junction with R54. Follow the tarmac round left onto this (Minninglow Lane), and continue along to the junction at SK 193 577 at the top (**The Nook**).

This is a good place to break the route if a **shorter version** is required – head downhill to the car park and pick up the HPT back to

81

↑ map continued from p78   ↓ map continues on p82

Middleton, then follow the final point of this route to return to Wirksworth – or start here (The Nook) and do the other half of the route!

Cross over onto the dirt track ahead, signposted to Biggin, and follow this uphill. After about 400m the track bends left. You need to follow an unclear waymarker right through the metal gate onto a stony track, which can be surprisingly awkward on a few of the short, steep and stony sections uphill.

This lane from The Nook to Cardle View is often referred to as **Cardlemere Lane**, however purists may insist Cardlemere Lane takes a 90° bend between Pikehall and Cardle View.

As you go through a metal gate, the track surface becomes a lot smoother and the gradient eases onto the plateau. Continue along this track (Cardlemere Lane) for a further 1km, descending very gently to another metal gate, where a 'Green Lane' cycleway joins from your right. Continue ahead on an even smoother surface for 1.4km to reach the A515 shortly before Biggin.

The easy bit of Cardlemere Lane

Road bikes will need to deviate at SK 193 577 via Parwich Hill, Dale End and Bigginmoor Farm to avoid Cardlemere Lane.

Turn right onto the rough but short cyclepath running alongside the A515, then almost immediately take a left turn onto a wide minor road signposted to Biggin. Cross under the TT bridge, and descend past the Waterloo Inn to a T-junction with Hardings Lane at the bottom of a hill, some 1.7km distant from the A515. Ignore the sharp left arm of the T, and continue right on R54 towards Heathcote.

Just 100m after this junction, take another dirt/gravel left track past Dale End House, and continue for 1.5km, initially uphill to a junction with a much rougher stonier track left.

Ignore that, and the right-joining track soon after, and continue on the fairly smooth dirt/gravel track which then descends (beware of bends and walkers) towards Hartington.

On joining a tarmac road turn left and head fairly steeply downhill for 500m past Hartington Hall, (now a youth hostel with café) into **Hartington**. At the T-junction you can detour left to reach the village green and alternative tea shops/pubs.

Turn right to head uphill out of Hartington towards Ashbourne on the B5054. After 1.2km you reach a crossroads. Turn left and head up **Long Dale**, signposted to Crowdecote. After 2.8km of very gentle climbing Hyde Lane joins you from the left. Ignore this and continue a further 700m to a junction right towards Parsley Hay. Take this, and after 800m you go under an old railway bridge, (carrying the HPT). Turn left 100m after this to enter **Parsley Hay** car park, where there is a visitor centre.

Turn left onto HPT back towards High Peak Junction to **Middleton Top**, which is some 18km south-east from here. Your only navigation is required after 400m, where the trail branches. Take the left fork, signposted as PBW.

ROUTE 10

BAKEWELL LOOP VIA HARTINGTON

Distance	42km
Total ascent/descent	850m
Grade	Moderate
Surface	86% road, 4% trail, 10% off-road
Start/finish	A6/A619 Roundabout in Central Bakewell SK 218 685
Parking	There are pay and display (£4 all day) and on-road parking options around Station Road, reached by following the A619 north towards Baslow, and turning right immediately over the river bridge
Cycle hire	Nearest is at Hassop Station (1.6km N on Monsal Trail)
Road Bikes?	OK with large detour at High Needham

Undulating route on mostly quiet lanes with a few steep hills, but rideable even in wet conditions.

From the roundabout, initially take A6 towards Matlock, but after only 20m turn right onto the B5055 towards Monyash (King Street). Head quite steeply uphill for 400m past the large All Saints parish church.

Turn left into Yeld Road and continue, still fairly steeply, uphill for 500m. Bend right past the cemetery entrance; the gradient eases past Lady Manners school playground and the road becomes Shutts Lane at the final houses.

Continue ahead here towards Youlgrave. The lane dips then continues past Noton Barn Farm, gently contouring for 1.7km before the beginning of the steep and twisty descent (very steep on hairpin) to the narrow Conksbury Bridge. Take care, even though the bridge crossing has been designated a Quiet Lane.

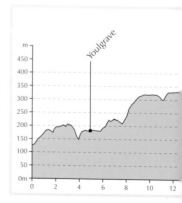

The lane rises up a steepening gradient on the far side; after roughly 300m turn left onto a narrow lane towards Youlgrave. Continue along this for roughly 1.1km to reach a crossroads in the centre of **Youlgrave** by the George PH. Turn right here along Main Street, passing the Bulls Head hotel and a stone fountain.

This sculptured **stone fountain**, a reservoir of 1500 gallons capacity, was erected in 1829 to provide the village with its first piped water supply from a nearby spring.

Continue out of the village past some allotments, where the

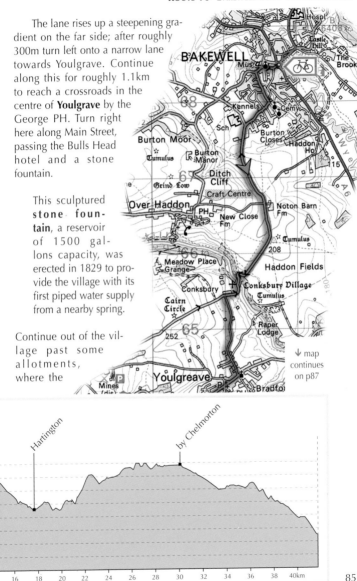

↓ map continues on p87

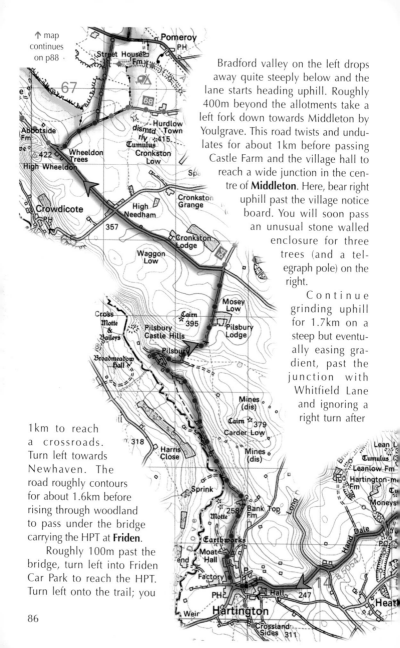

Bradford valley on the left drops away quite steeply below and the lane starts heading uphill. Roughly 400m beyond the allotments take a left fork down towards Middleton by Youlgrave. This road twists and undulates for about 1km before passing Castle Farm and the village hall to reach a wide junction in the centre of **Middleton**. Here, bear right uphill past the village notice board. You will soon pass an unusual stone walled enclosure for three trees (and a telegraph pole) on the right.

Continue grinding uphill for 1.7km on a steep but eventually easing gradient, past the junction with Whitfield Lane and ignoring a right turn after

1km to reach a crossroads. Turn left towards Newhaven. The road roughly contours for about 1.6km before rising through woodland to pass under the bridge carrying the HPT at **Friden**.

Roughly 100m past the bridge, turn left into Friden Car Park to reach the HPT. Turn left onto the trail; you

↑ map continues on p88

will pass over two gated farm access tracks, and after about 1.7km come to a third gated track.

Turn sharp left up this initially steep and stony track which soon eases in both respects. The next 400m is relatively short, but can be moderately difficult. Cross the A515, with the Jug and Glass inn visible 150m to your left, to gain a moderately steep and loose downhill.

Turn right onto the road at the end of the stony track, and descend under the TT (PBW) viaduct 300m later. Continue straight ahead past a couple of side roads to descend gently down Hand Dale into **Hartington** to reach a wide open junction in the centre of the village. Hartington holds a few pubs/tea rooms for the weary!

From the village centre turn right towards Pilsbury (gated road) and past the duckpond on R54C. This lane threads the very pretty upper reaches of the valley of the River Dove for about 3.5km, passing Bank Top Farm among others. **Pilsbury** itself is only a couple of farms, after which the road abruptly turns right for a steep climb up the hillside (Waggon Low). After about 1km the climb eases, and you pass Pilsbury Lodge farm on your right, descending gently for about 600m to a crossroads.

Turn left onto a more major road heading towards

← map continued from p85

Crowdecote, and once you have ground stead- ily up a moderate hill for 500m the gradient eases for the next 1.3km. Cross over a more major road in the little hamlet of High Needham towards Earl Sterndale,

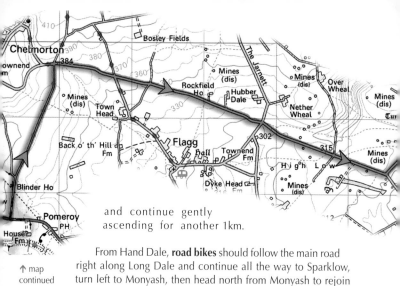

and continue gently ascending for another 1km.

↑ map continued from p 86

From Hand Dale, **road bikes** should follow the main road right along Long Dale and continue all the way to Sparklow, turn left to Monyash, then head north from Monyash to rejoin the route at SK 148 689.

Descend past **Wheeldon Trees** farm but don't get carried away with the descent, as roughly 200m beyond this farm, there's a sharp right turn. Take this to follow R68 moderately steeply uphill on a tarmac track, then gently downhill to a dip below some power lines. Immediately beyond the wires, turn left onto a well surfaced stony track which leads gently uphill.

Looking back down the lane leading up Waggon Low

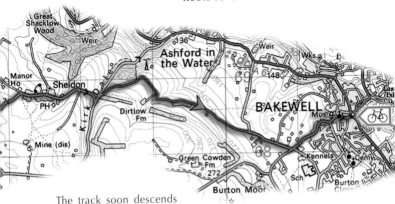

The track soon descends past a large quarry and the end of the HPT before rising moderately to the A515. Here, turn right following the PBW on a segregated trail on the right side of the busy road for 250m. When the segregating wooden fence ends, turn left across the A515 and into a narrow county lane heading down towards Chelmorton.

Pass Blinder House on the left, and take a stony track (PBW) heading off right as the road bends very gently left. The track surface is initially good, and although it deteriorates slightly after 500m (after a farm field track leaves it), it's still reasonable in wet conditions.

At the end of the track, just outside **Chelmorton**, turn right at a junction towards Sheldon. Follow this road straight ahead for about 5km, ignoring all side roads. At the end of a long straight, with Magpie Mine visible on the hillside ahead, turn left to climb gently to Sheldon on a narrow lane. Descend steeply through **Sheldon** village past the Cock and Pullet PH. Pass good views over the Wye Valley, and continue steeply downhill to reach a T-junction.

Turn left down Kirkdale towards Ashford, and roughly 100m later fork right and steeply uphill on a narrow country lane (unsuitable for HGVs). The gradient eases fairly quickly, and then descends gradually for 2.3km with fine views over the Wye valley. Take care at bends and a rough section early on. Later, ignore a left turn for Ashford and a second left turn immediately after Pennine Paving to reach the B5055. Turn left onto this and head steeply downhill into **Bakewell**.

You will recognise the final part of your descent as being your initial ascent up King Street. At the bottom you cannot turn right, and must instead go left and around the roundabout if required.

ROUTE 11

LEEK LOOP VIA THE ROACHES

Distance	43km
Total ascent/descent	989m
Grade	Moderate
Surface	95% road, 5% trail
Start/finish	Vicarage Road Car Park (actually on Ball Haye Road) SJ 987 568
Getting to the start	Close to junction of A53 and A523 in Leek town centre
Parking	The car park is operated by Staffordshire Moorlands DC (☎ 01538 395674). Open 8am–6pm each day, pay and display 9.30am–3.30pm: 2010 charges were £1.50 for 3–6hrs
Cycle Hire	Two hire centres in Waterhouses, 14km south of Hulme End, via the Manifold Valley Trail (see Route 11)
Road bikes?	Reasonable

Hilly route on country lanes crossing Morridge and the Roaches. Good views from upper sections.

From the car park exit, turn left up Vicarage road, bearing right at the park gates. Gently climb the road ahead, passing Ball Haye Tavern, and shortly afterwards bear right along Novi Lane opposite Moorlands Dental Practice. Follow this lane through a housing estate and up a short steep rise to the A53 at the end. Turn left onto the main road, and then bear right at the Moss Rose Inn towards Thorncliffe 200m later.

Descend for 300m towards a stream bridge. Just before the bridge, turn right onto a lane, ascending after Freshwinds Farm, and ignoring a lane to the left at the head of the first rise. The road levels out after **Lark**

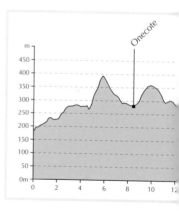

90

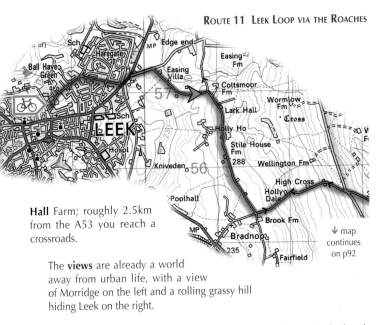

Hall Farm; roughly 2.5km from the A53 you reach a crossroads.

↓ map
continues
on p92

The **views** are already a world away from urban life, with a view of Morridge on the left and a rolling grassy hill hiding Leek on the right.

Turn left onto a more major road towards Onecote, which soon leads sharply downhill past a bend to cross a stream followed by a long steep uphill. Continuing past Holly Dale farm on the steepest section, the gradient eases to High Cross house, and the end of the pull uphill to **Morridge** is almost in sight.

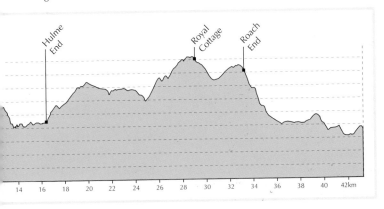

Rise up a final steep section to reach Blakelow Road.

Dog-leg right then left into Douse Lane and enjoy a well-earned long descent for 2.5km into **Onecote** village. Turn left onto the B5053 towards Warslow at the road-end T-junction.

Cross a narrow river bridge by the Jervis Arms PH, and begin a long moderate ascent shortly after passing a side-turn to Home Farm. The gradient up Butterton Moor eases as a side-turn from Grindon joins from the right. Continue along for roughly 500m further, and as the road starts to descend, turn right towards Butterton, descending steeply into the village past the general store. In **Butterton**, follow all options leftwards and head towards Ecton, via Penhooks Lane, Church Lane and Waste Lane, passing by the church on your right.

Enjoy 2km of steepening descent on a winding country lane towards Swainsley Hall. (Don't enjoy the final part too much or you'll miss the turn!) Shortly after an unusual stone parapet on the left, take a sharp left turn back

↑ map continues on p95

→ map continued from p91

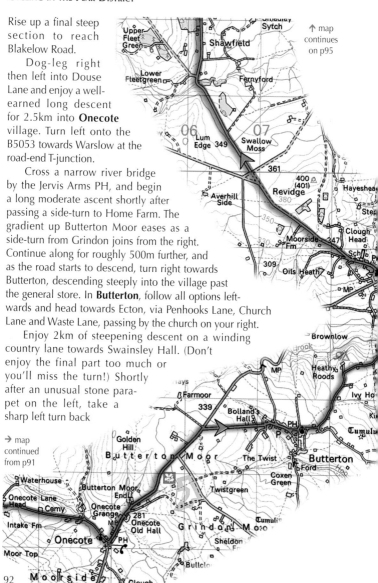

92

on yourself, signposted Manifold Valley. Take this for 50m until it turns left into a tunnel.

Don't go into the tunnel, but instead turn right onto a car-free tarmac track, soon passing through a narrow wooden gate onto the Manifold Trail. Follow this trail for roughly 1.4km to the trail end car park in **Hulme End** (café), taking care at a road crossing in roughly 800m. Exit the car park left onto the main road, ignoring the sign for R54.

Roughly 300m later, turn left by Cowlow farm up a rough tarmac road, with an initial steep climb. The gradient eases past a roofless stone barn, and descends from Cliff House Farm to the T-junction at the end of Cawlow Lane. Turn right here and continue for 50m before turning left to gain the B5053 as it enters **Warslow**.

Turn right 250m later onto Leek Road, heading uphill past the Greyhound Inn. Continue ascending for 2.1km, past the school and over a cattle grid, to reach a side-turn right as main road bends left. Take this right, and in 150m cross a more major road into a narrowing lane.

Continue along for 1.25km, descending gently to a stream bridge just after a bend right. Continue straight ahead past 'Hayshead', avoiding a side turn left to stay on the 'main' lane, heading

Family of cyclists on the Manifold Trail just after the Ecton tunnel

gently uphill. The lane then roughly contours for 1.7km into **Newtown**.

Turn right at the lane end towards Longnor, and in roughly 100m fork left down a single track lane (unsuitable for long vehicles). Turn left at the cross-roads and descend moderately steeply to a ford (usually dry).

Rise up quite steeply past Oakenclough Farm ignoring a side-turn right by **Oakenclough Hall**. Continue rising moderately to the lane end some 1.2km from the ford. Turn left onto a more major road where the views over the high plateau open up.

The road ahead climbs overall towards the A53, but is broken up by descents and steep ascents. As the spiky rocks of Hen Cloud

↓ map continues on p96

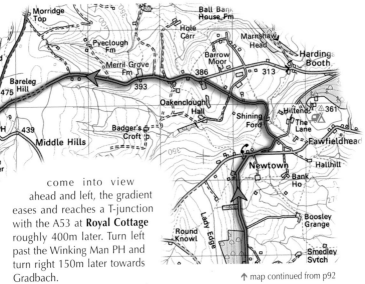

↑ map continued from p92

come into view ahead and left, the gradient eases and reaches a T-junction with the A53 at **Royal Cottage** roughly 400m later. Turn left past the Winking Man PH and turn right 150m later towards Gradbach.

Descend moderately steeply, bearing left at a triangular junction, soon passing **Hazel Barrow** kennels. Bear right at a fork to embark on a wide sweeping circuit of the head of the Black Brook valley, and over a cattle grid. At the far side the road climbs gently, beyond a slight summit, to reach another cattle grid at **Roach End** 3.5km from the main road.

Now start a steep descent with a great view down to Tittesworth Reservoir. Descend cautiously at first, this road can be busy in peak times, and a gate across the road after roughly 400m is awkward to stop for if going fast.

The gradient eases significantly after the gate until a side-turn right by a stone water trough. Turn right towards Meerbrook down a very steep, narrow and twisting lane. Once past the turn to Brownsett farm the road straightens and gradient eases – ironically allowing much faster speeds! **Meerbrook** village is reached, outside the Lazy Trout PH, about 4km from Roach End.

A detour of 500m left to the **Tittesworth Reservoir visitor centre** (café, toilets) may be worthwhile.

Turn right towards Rushton, then 80m later left towards Leek. Continue gently up this road, initially running parallel to the reservoir, before bending right and moderately uphill to Park House farm.

View over rolling dales near Royal Cottage

Descend fairly steeply after the farm; the lane then undulates past Upper Foker farm. Continue straight ahead, descending fairly steeply to pass the Abbey Inn in **Abbey Green**. Cross a river bridge and bend right on the outskirts of Leek.

Just after the 30mph sign, turn left into Park Road by the pine mill. Continue straight ahead, climbing a moderate gradient, to reach a gate across the road at the entrance to Brough Park. Go through A-bars to join the continuation road through the park, which gently bends right and soon gently downhill to leave the park at grand iron gates. Continue straight ahead from the gates and turn right into Vicarage Road Car Park at the bottom of the dip.

↓ map continued from p94

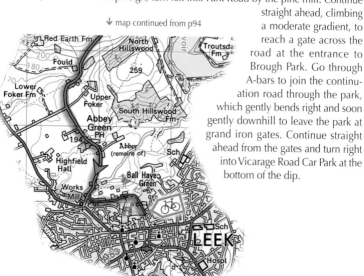

ROUTE 12

WATERHOUSES LOOP VIA MORRIDGE AND LONGNOR

Distance	44km
Total ascent/descent	820m
Grade	Moderate
Surface	77% road, 23% trail
Start/Finish	Manifold Trail Car Park in Waterhouses village SK 084 501
Parking	The car park is owned by the Peak District National Park, and is pay and display 10am–6pm every day: current charges (2010) are £3.50/day
Cycle hire	Available at the start of the route from either Manifold Valley Cycle Hire, or Brown End Farm Cycle Hire
Road bikes?	Reasonable

An easy way to gain good height on Morridge, with a gentle return on the Manifold Trail.

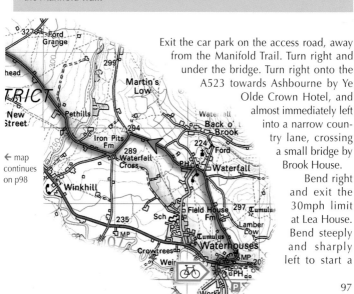

Exit the car park on the access road, away from the Manifold Trail. Turn right and under the bridge. Turn right onto the A523 towards Ashbourne by Ye Olde Crown Hotel, and almost immediately left into a narrow country lane, crossing a small bridge by Brook House.

Bend right and exit the 30mph limit at Lea House. Bend steeply and sharply left to start a

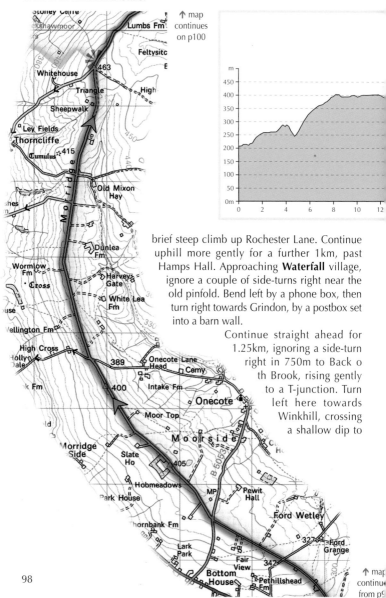

↑ map continues on p100

brief steep climb up Rochester Lane. Continue uphill more gently for a further 1km, past Hamps Hall. Approaching **Waterfall** village, ignore a couple of side-turns right near the old pinfold. Bend left by a phone box, then turn right towards Grindon, by a postbox set into a barn wall.

Continue straight ahead for 1.25km, ignoring a side-turn right in 750m to Back o th Brook, rising gently to a T-junction. Turn left here towards Winkhill, crossing a shallow dip to

↑ map continues from p9

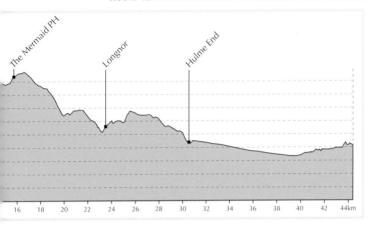

reach a minor crossroads by a farm. Turn right towards Ford and enjoy a 600m descent past Iron Pits Farm to a narrow bridge (risk of flooding).

Rise up the far side, initially moderately steeply, to start the long ascent up to Morridge. Continue straight ahead on a 1km long 1 in 13 ascent past **Pethills** farm; the gradient eases significantly by Pethills Bank Cottage. Continue for a further 200m to cross over Ford Road onto another country lane, passing many hay meadows full of grass and wildflowers.

At the end of Fairview Road, some 1.1km later, cross the B5053 at a staggered crossroads onto Blakelow Road, rising moderately gently again to stay running along **Morridge** ridgeline. Continue straight ahead past Birdsgrove Farm, and now it really becomes obvious that you are running along a high undulating ridge overlooking deep and wide valleys either side. Continue along this ridgeline road for roughly 6km, ignoring all side-turns and passing a small covered reservoir (1.3km), Dunlea Farm (3.8km), New Mixon Hay Farm (4.3km) and New Sheepwalk Farm (5.5km). The road rises moderately uphill at the end to reach a T-junction.

Many fields along side this ridge-line road have fluffy blobs of white shimmering down - this is **bog cotton grass** – a marsh-loving upland grass.

Turn right here onto a busier road to continue undulating along the ridge line, with excellent views of The Roaches, Hen Cloud and Ramshaw Rocks across the valley to the left.

The Roaches are a prominent **gritstone outcrop** that forms part of the western edge of the Peak District.

Enjoy a gentle descent, before climb-ing gradually past the Mermaid Inn PH, ignoring the right turn

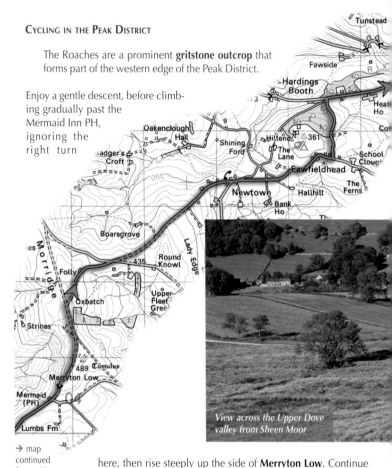

View across the Upper Dove valley from Sheen Moor

→ map continued from p98

here, then rise steeply up the side of **Merryton Low**. Continue straight ahead past a side-turn right beside the Mermaid's pool, and 500m later fork right towards Newtown, some 3km distant. Enjoy the descent on this country lane, continuing straight ahead over a crossroads in 1km. A further 1km later, the gradient increases past Boarsgrove farm for a fur-ther 1.3km. Continue through **Newtown** village, avoiding the right turn at the phone box, and bearing right at a fork 100m later, cross a shallow valley and rise to Hall Hill farm.

Turn left on top of a slight rise 700m later, just beyond a stone farmhouse. Descend past Hill Wood to reach a T-junction with a more major road. Turn

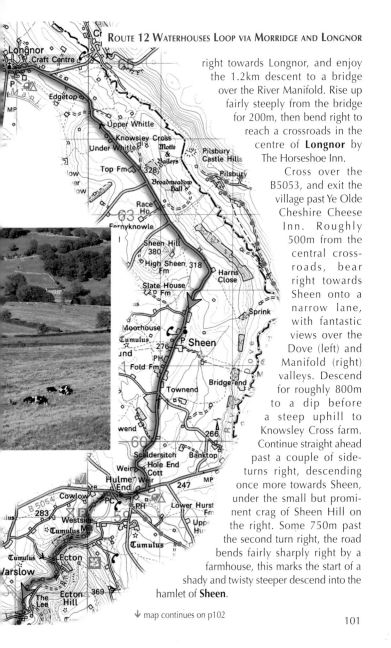

right towards Longnor, and enjoy the 1.2km descent to a bridge over the River Manifold. Rise up fairly steeply from the bridge for 200m, then bend right to reach a crossroads in the centre of **Longnor** by The Horseshoe Inn.

Cross over the B5053, and exit the village past Ye Olde Cheshire Cheese Inn. Roughly 500m from the central cross-roads, bear right towards Sheen onto a narrow lane, with fantastic views over the Dove (left) and Manifold (right) valleys. Descend for roughly 800m to a dip before a steep uphill to Knowsley Cross farm. Continue straight ahead past a couple of side-turns right, descending once more towards Sheen, under the small but prominent crag of Sheen Hill on the right. Some 750m past the second turn right, the road bends fairly sharply right by a farmhouse, this marks the start of a shady and twisty steeper descend into the hamlet of **Sheen**.

↓ map continues on p102

101

The very grand village hall, old school house and old coach house suggest that this **hamlet** once held a more prestigious role in Derbyshire than today, but the settlement is also larger than it first appears, with a second area of housing roughly 200m further south from the impressive-sounding The Palace Farm.

Continue straight ahead over a crossroads on Pown Street, and enjoy a 1km long and somewhat twisty descent to cross a tributary of the River Manifold. Rise briefly uphill to reach a T-junction with the B5054. Turn right and descend to **Hulme End**, forking right over a stone river bridge towards the Manifold Valley Visitor Centre. Turn left into the Manifold Trail Car park (loos, café) and bear right at the end of the car park onto the Manifold Trail.

The Manifold valley used to be important for **copper mining**, with a major mine at Ecton.

Continue straight ahead along the tarmac track back to Waterhouses some 14km distant. Although generally traffic free, beware of a number of unsigned road cross-

↓ map
continued
from p101

Cyclist on Rocester Lane, Waterhouses

ings with unclear priorities, and sections of the trail which are also a public road.

> Notable features along the way include a 200m long tunnel (2.5km), Wettonmill café (4 km), Thor's Cave (6km), **Weag's Barn** nature reserve (8.5km) and Lea Hurst Farm café (11.5km). The end of the trail is marked by a short rise over the last of many river bridges, with Brown End Farm Cycle Hire on your right.
>
> There are two unusual features of the 'Manifold Valley'. Firstly, not all of of it belongs to the Manifold itself. For the first two-thirds of the trail, you are indeed gradually descending the Manifold Valley; however, just beyond Weag's Bridge, you are turned right up the tributary valley of the River Hamps. This river is notable for being 'dry' for much of the year, due to the porous limestone bedrock, giving rise to many bridge crossings of a non-existent river!

Cross the A523 and bear right along a cycle path running along the far verge. Turn left (dismount) and under the bridge where the trail ends and continue up the slope for roughly 100m to reach a narrow tarmac track. Turn sharp left to return to the car park in **Waterhouses** some 200m later.

ROUTE 13

PENISTONE LOOP VIA HOLMFIRTH	
Distance	38km
Total ascent/descent	875m
Grade	Moderate
Surface	57% road, 31 % trail, 11% off-road
Start/finish	Penistone railway station SE 251 033
Parking	Limited free parking is available on station access road or in free car park 200m west of the station on Shrewsbury Road
Cycle hire	None nearby – see Appendix A
Road bikes?	Reasonable with detours to avoid High Bank Lane and Cartworth Moor Road

Over the high northern edges of the Peak District (both east and west) with an easy finish via the TPT.

In Penistone Station car park, locate an easily missed tarmac path immediately to the right of the station building. This reaches the TPT in 15m. Turn right along it. After about 2km along this easy trail, you reach a crossing of rough track, where rails are still visible in the ground. Turn sharp right, and right again onto a minor tarmac road running parallel to the trail. Follow this for 500m, to reach a junction with the A628 on the edge of **Thurlstone**.

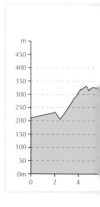

Turn left along the main road, and after 300m, at the crest of the first rise, bear right into High Bank Lane. Climb this narrow lane for 2km, losing the tarmac in favour of a stone surface higher up, to return to tarmac opposite a T-junction at the top. Turn left up Royd Moor Hill, which soon drops to another T-junction after 200m. Turn right to regain the ridge, passing close by the wind turbines on your right, to reach a three-way junction on Whitley Common after 2.5km.

Turn left at this junction, and then after 150m turn right into a minor lane which retains its altitude. Follow this for 800m to reach a crossroads where a more major road joins from the left. Continue straight ahead, then bear right at a triangular junction. Pass over Windmill Lane at a crossroads, and then descend for 1.5km to reach a five-way crossroads at **Lane Head**.

Turn left up Wall Nook Gate. Rise gently past some houses, then avoid two left forks as the road begins to descend, steep and twisting, to reach a staggered junction by the Crossroads Inn. Cross over the A635 onto Horn Lane, towards Snowgate Head.

Turn right onto Acre Lane at a triangular junction. After 300m the road bends sharply left and becomes Ebson House Lane. Continue descending this narrow and twisty lane to reach the hamlet of **Fulstone**. Turn left at the T-junction onto Fulstone Hall Lane and descend gently for 1.5km into **New**

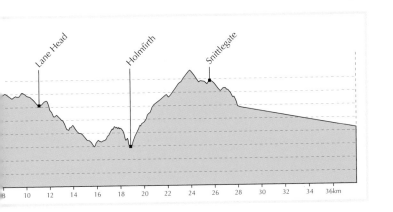

← map
continues
on p107

Mill. Turn right at the T-junction by the large church to steeply descend to the main road.

Turn right along the A635 for 100m, to reach a T-junction with the A616 opposite the Duke of Leeds PH. Turn right towards Manchester, then turn left towards Totties. Head steeply uphill, and bear right into Royds Avenue where the gradient eases significantly. Continue straight ahead for 800m through a housing estate to reach the end of the road opposite a school.

Turn left and head briefly but steeply uphill before bending right as a one-way side-road joins from the left. Ignore the next left (Pell Lane), then fork left immediately onto Lower Town End Road. Continue straight ahead for 400m past several side-roads to reach Cliff Road on the left. Fork left onto this and rise quite steeply. Fantastic views over the valley below.

After 550m, fork right onto Cliff Lane and head downhill for 600m – it's steep and narrow after Highfield Studio. Turn left at the road end, ignoring a narrow lane right (Bunkers Hill) after 100m. Continue to reach the road end on a very sharp angled junction. Turn right and head steeply down this narrow lane (South Lane) to reach the centre of **Holmfirth**.

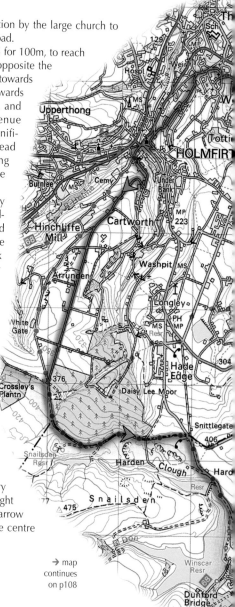

→ map continues on p108

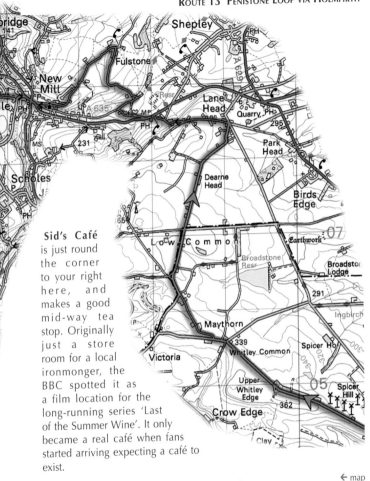

Sid's Café is just round the corner to your right here, and makes a good mid-way tea stop. Originally just a store room for a local ironmonger, the BBC spotted it as a film location for the long-running series 'Last of the Summer Wine'. It only became a real café when fans started arriving expecting a café to exist.

← map continued from p105

Turn right onto Dunford Road then the next few junctions all follow immediately on from each other. Turn left onto Town Gate (A635), fork left by Barclays Bank onto the rightmost of two narrow lanes (Hollowgate), and past a couple of fish and chip shops. Turn left up New Fold, which leads to the very steep and narrow Goose Green.

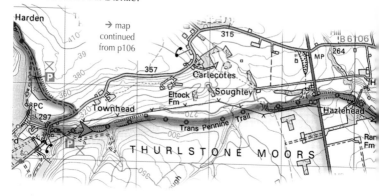

Bikes with narrow tyres might find this next off-road section awkward. To avoid it, turn right at the top of Goose Green (SE 142 081), left at SE 131 074, and continue steadily uphill to rejoin the route at the end of Cartworth Moor Road (SE 130 050).

At the top of Goose Green you reach a junction with Cartworth Road and Cemetery Road. Turn left then immediately right to continue steeply up Cartworth Road for roughly 500m. After fields open out on the left and the gradient has eased, take a sharp right turn into an unsigned rough track. Follow this initially uphill to regain tarmac at a crossroads in roughly 1.3km.

On Cartworth Moor Road

Continue straight ahead over the crossroads up Cartworth Moor Road. After Moorfield 'Mistake' Farm the route becomes a stony and potholed byway but remains easy-going for roughly 1km, crossing over a vehicle track roughly half-way. At the end junction, turn left onto a country lane, past a coniferous planta-tion. Continue moderately uphill for roughly 900m, then enjoy the 1.5km long moderate descent to a crossroads near **Snittlegate**.

Turn right at the crossroads, following R68 signs, first climbing and then descending for 2.1km past Winscar Reservoir to the end of the road. Turn right and downhill to **Dunford Bridge**. At the bottom of the dip, turn left into the TPT car park and pass through this to join the TPT. Follow the TPT for 10km to return to Penistone Station.

Near Snittlegate with small reservoir in background

109

ROUTE 14

TIDESWELL LOOP VIA PEAK FOREST

Distance	31km
Total ascent/descent	580m
Grade	Moderate
Surface	88% road, 12% off-road
Start/finish	By Cathedral of the Peak – Tideswell village centre SK 152 757
Parking	Free on-street parking is available in the centre of the village
Cycle hire	Available from Trail Monkeys, Bradwell
Road bikes?	Detour required at Eldon Hill Quarries

Goes through the heart of limestone country – watch out for the hills, but enjoy several long gentle descents.

Leaving Tideswell church (known as the 'Cathedral of the Peak') on your right, bend right then left around Natwest Bank and continue southwards out of the village on Buxton Road for roughly 500m (passing a piano showroom). Keep going for 100m further, then turn right at a both-ways fork in the road, into a narrow lane (Richard Lane). Continue moderately uphill for 250m, passing a busy local haulage depot on the left. Turn left at the T-junction onto a narrow country lane, which in places feels to be little more than a tarmac track.

After roughly 1km keep left at another T-junction, and descend on this road for 1.2km into **Miller's Dale**. It gets increasingly steep after the Monks Retreat Holiday Cottages driveway – this is not the place to discover problems with your brakes, Turn right onto the B6049.

It's worth a quick detour left in 50m to see the **Miller's Dale Meal Mill Wheel**. (Try saying that after a few pints of the local beer!)

Continue ahead under the old double railway viaduct to reach a side-turn right to Wormhill. Take this and grind slowly uphill past the Monsal Trail car park.

Just before the bend left at Glebe House Farm, look back towards the viaduct to see the old **lime kilns** of the railway era. Another pleasant detour in late spring/early summer is along the footpath at the bend – the **wildflowers** near the start of the descent into Monks Dale are often fantastic.

Bend left past Glebe House Farm and continue steadily but more gently uphill for roughly 1km. The road then levels out briefly before undulating past The Barn Studio, to reach **Wormhill**. Continue gently uphill for a further 100m to pass the elliptical shaped village green, complete with Ye Olde Stocks, then continue uphill for a further 800m, passing two turns for the Pennine Bridleway, either side of Old Hall Farm.

There is a memorial to **James Brindley** almost hidden in the shrubbery on the village green. He was a well-known local engineer whose achievements include the Chesterfield Canal (Route 1).

Continue past a minor summit of the road, then bend left at a junction of small roads towards Peak Forest. Continue for 800m, then take the second right, again towards Peak Forest. Continue for 3.2km, initially rising gently before a very pleasant 2km descent on a wide but quiet country lane.

↑ map continues on p112

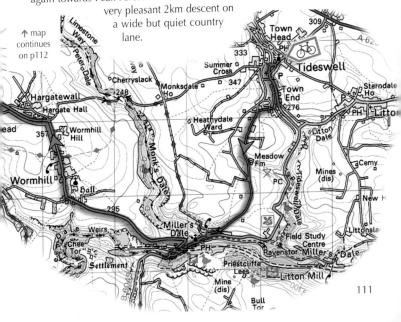

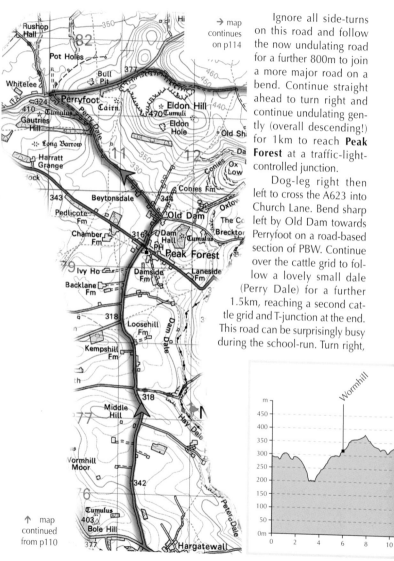

→ map
continues
on p114

Ignore all side-turns on this road and follow the now undulating road for a further 800m to join a more major road on a bend. Continue straight ahead to turn right and continue undulating gently (overall descending!) for 1km to reach **Peak Forest** at a traffic-light-controlled junction.

Dog-leg right then left to cross the A623 into Church Lane. Bend sharp left by Old Dam towards Perryfoot on a road-based section of PBW. Continue over the cattle grid to follow a lovely small dale (Perry Dale) for a further 1.5km, reaching a second cattle grid and T-junction at the end. This road can be surprisingly busy during the school-run. Turn right,

↑ map
continued
from p110

Open view across hay meadows, typical of White Peak near Wormhill and Peak Forest

continuing for 1.3km, steeply at first. Continue past a small lake, part of Eldon Hill Quarry, then turn right onto a stone track through a large wooden gate.

Alternative route in wet conditions – continue straight ahead for 1.7km, then turn right 150m after Oxlow House onto a 1.5km long gentler track

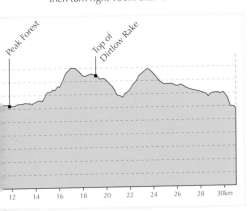

past Rowter Farm to avoid most of the off-road hill. **Road bikes** may need to descend all the way into Castleton via Winnats Pass, and up a road leading through Pin Dale and beside the Dirtlow Rake track to rejoin the road at SK146 814.

Continue uphill for 1.2km on a mostly gravel surface,

→ map
continued
from p112

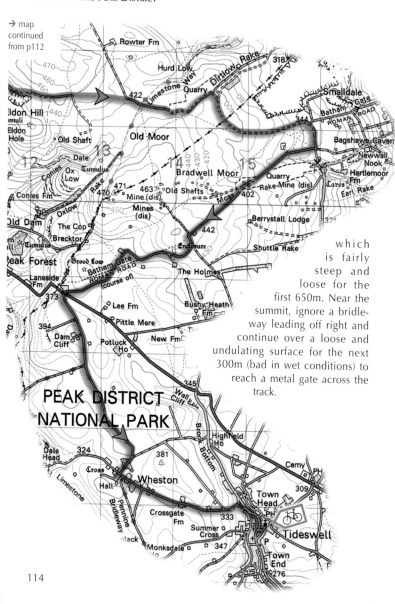

which
is fairly
steep and
loose for the
first 650m. Near the
summit, ignore a bridle-
way leading off right and
continue over a loose and
undulating surface for the next
300m (bad in wet conditions) to
reach a metal gate across the
track.

The strange lumpy depressions in the fields either side of the track are almost certainly characteristic remnants of small-scale **lead mining**, undertaken by crofters as a way of supplementing their meagre farming income in the 17th century.

The next 350m can be somewhat rough and loose in places. It's never too bad for too long, but those new to off-road riding may be intimidated by parts of the terrain on this and the following 400m section. Continue gently downhill on stony vehicle tracks until another farm track joins from the left. Continue straight ahead on a smoother surface for 600m, and cross the Limestone Way. Continue gently uphill on a good stone surface to a final metal gate.

Ignore a field access track left and continue straight ahead for 250m to gain the plateau summit. Shortly after, the track bends left by an information board, continue for 350m and the track bends slightly right. At the next bend in 100m (slightly left) turn right through a gateway to reach a country lane. If the track gets loose and very rough, you've gone too far and are descending Dirtlow Rake – turn round and look for the exit on your left.

Technically speaking the **rights of way** over this short section off the track linking Dirtlow Rake to the road are not clear. In practice it is well-used by riders and it is unlikely that you will encounter problems using it, but if challenged be prepared to walk down Dirtlow Rake (or ride it if you can!) instead to gain the country lane running parallel some 1km further downhill.

Cyclists on the track above Dirtlow Rake

Turn right onto this country lane, and follow it briefly uphill. The uphill soon ends and becomes a thoroughly enjoyable 1.5km descent, steepening as it goes, to reach a long sweeping bend right past the cement works entrance.

Turn right onto another narrow country lane, roughly 450m after the works exit (well before a long quarry ahead). Take this gently uphill for 2.2km. This lane steepens where it effectively cuts the quarry in two, before running over Bradwell Moor. Bend left then right near the summit and descend for 2.45km to reach the A623. This lane roughly follows the line of Batham Gate – an old Roman Road.

Rejoin the Limestone Way on a country lane, and continue along this to Wheston. The initial ascent soon gives way to another 2.5km-long gentle descent. Turn left at the road end in **Wheston**, ignoring the PBW and other side-turns, then descend for 2km further into Tideswell. As you come into **Tideswell**, the road ends steeply. The 'cathedral' spire makes a good guidemarker back to the centre of the village. Turn right, and bend right past the Star Inn to reach another junction opposite the Natwest Bank. Turn left by the bank to regain your start point.

Cathedral in the Peak, Tideswell, Peak District National Park

ROUTE 15

BUXTON LOOP VIA BAKEWELL

Distance	48km
Total ascent/descent	1050m
Grade	Hard
Surface	69% road, 27% trail, 4% off-road
Start/finish	Buxton railway station SK 060 737
Parking	Buxton railway station has a small car park that is available for non rail-users (pay and display, £4 a day), but the nearby larger Pavilion Gardens car park may offer a better chance of spaces.
Cycle hire	Nearest available is at Hassop Station (near Bakewell)
Road bikes?	Narrow wheeled bikes are not suitable for the bridleway sections (eg Pennine BW), the bridleway the link at the end of the HPT or if the Litton Tunnel avoidance route is required.

A hilly route that exits industrial Buxton over rural limestone hills to the Monsal Trail, for an easy section to Bakewell. Return is via a hilly but scenic route – with a great view over Hitter, Parkhouse and Chrome Hills

At the time of writing, it is expected that the Monsal Trail Tunnels extension will be complete by Easter 2011, and further extensions are expected on both the Monsal Trail via Woodale and the High Peak Trail from Harpur Hill via Ladmanlow/Staker Hill during the next few years. The route description here uses some of the new Tunnels, but the ideal route will obviously change as things on the ground change. (So it may be a good idea to check the updates section of the Cicerone website before using this route!) If route-deviation issues are met on the ground, then you would be best to follow the official signs.

Do **not** attempt to take a cycle down the Chee Valley from Wyedale – it's a very tough path on foot even without carrying a bike!

Exiting from Buxton Rail Station, turn left onto Station Road and head downhill and straight over a roundabout by Aldi. Turn left at the next roundabout and under a railway viaduct towards Matlock. Turn left at the next roundabout onto the **A6**, heading northwards towards Stockport.

Grind steadily up this road for roughly 800m,

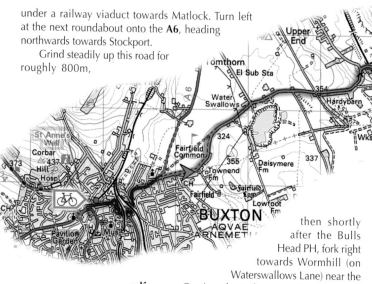

then shortly after the Bulls Head PH, fork right towards Wormhill (on Waterswallows Lane) near the **golf course**. Continue for 1.6km to reach a T-junction. Here turn right and continue for 1.8km descending steeply past Tunstead Quarry, to cross a **rail bridge** by the Tarmac works.

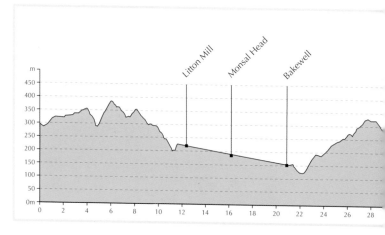

Continue uphill, steeply at first, for roughly 1.5km to reach a side-turn to **Tunstead** (only). Take this and shortly after a steeper descent on a bend right, follow Pennine Bridleway (PBW) signs left onto a track towards Wormhill. Continue along this for

→ map continues on p120

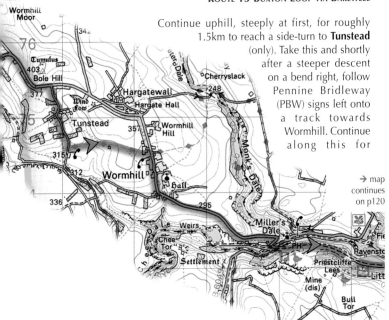

1.2km and through Old Hall Farm (very slippery and often mucky when wet) to gain the road at the edge of **Wormhill**.

Turn right and follow the road for roughly 2.6km down into **Miller's Dale**, to reach the Monsal Trail **car park**. Turn right into this and continue past the left side of the old station buildings to gain the trail. Turn left onto this, and you should now be able to continue along for nearly 11km to reach **Bakewell Station**.

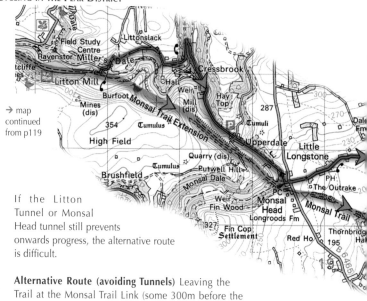

→ map
continued
from p119

If the Litton
Tunnel or Monsal
Head tunnel still prevents
onwards progress, the alternative route
is difficult.

Alternative Route (avoiding Tunnels) Leaving the
Trail at the Monsal Trail Link (some 300m before the
Litton tunnel), you are now required to dismount

*The distinctive lone chimney
on the stiff climb to Cressbrook (alternative route)*

(footpath only) over a steep, rocky and awkward descent which leads to a very narrow bridge over the River Wye. Cross this and follow the footpath to exit (right) onto the road in **Litton Mill** village where you may ride again. Bear left of the gateway to Litton Mill, and very steeply uphill for 100m past Meadow Hill House to reach a metal gate and footpath through a steep grassy dale.

The signs say 'Footpath' throughout the route from Litton Mill to the top of Cressbrook, but cyclists may ride it all due to old rights still remaining.

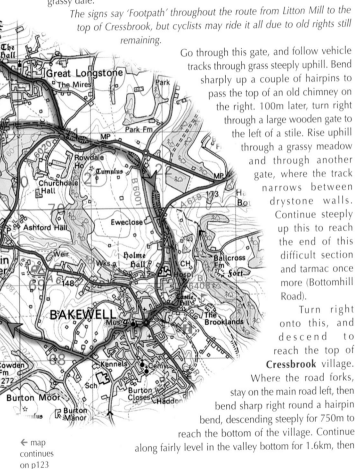

Go through this gate, and follow vehicle tracks through grass steeply uphill. Bend sharply up a couple of hairpins to pass the top of an old chimney on the right. 100m later, turn right through a large wooden gate to the left of a stile. Rise uphill through a grassy meadow and through another gate, where the track narrows between drystone walls. Continue steeply up this to reach the end of this difficult section and tarmac once more (Bottomhill Road).

Turn right onto this, and descend to reach the top of **Cressbrook** village. Where the road forks, stay on the main road left, then bend sharp right round a hairpin bend, descending steeply for 750m to reach the bottom of the village. Continue along fairly level in the valley bottom for 1.6km, then

← map continues on p123

The former Bakewell station on the Monsal Trail

← map
continues
on p125

face a steep 500m uphill to reach the viewpoint (and welcome pub/café!) at **Monsal Head**.

Dog-leg right then left over the more major road to enter **Little Longstone**. Bend right in the village and continue to **Great Longstone**. Continue past The Crispin PH along the main street,

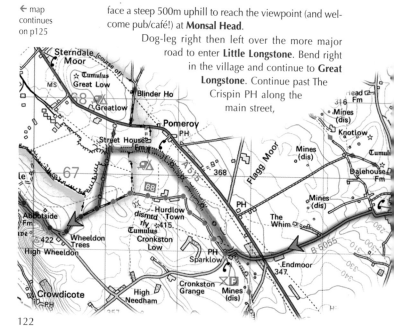

bending right as you leave the village. Roughly 600m later reach a road joining from the left, and gain the eastern section of the **Monsal Trail** via an access point at the start of this road. Turn left onto the trail and follow it for 3km past Hassop Station (café, cycle hire) to reach **Bakewell** Station.

Reaching Bakewell Station, bend right just before the station building to gain the car park. Cross this, and turn left onto the road, heading gently downhill to reach the A619 by the river bridge. Turn left along this, and follow the road through the one-way section to reach a major roundabout in the centre of town. This junction is awkward – turn left on the A6 towards Matlock, but immediately turn right towards Monyash and up King Street. Follow this steep road for 1.1km out of town to reach a rural crossroads.

← map continued from p121

Turn right towards Ashford and continue along this country lane for 3.1km (ignoring a side-turn right towards Ashford near an old guide stoop) to reach a more major road. Turn left and rise up Kirk Dale towards Flagg for 1.2km to reach a T-junction at the end of the road.

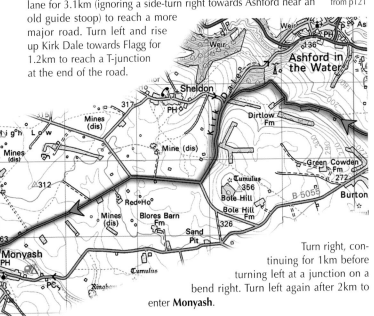

Turn right, continuing for 1km before turning left at a junction on a bend right. Turn left again after 2km to enter **Monyash**.

Guide stoops are forerunners of the modern signpost system, stone markers at junctions which were required by law from the very late 17th century onwards.

123

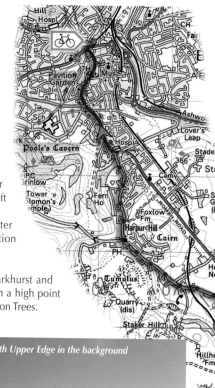

As you reach the village green (café, PH), turn right towards Buxton along the B5055, continuing steadily uphill for 2km to reach A515. Cross this busy road with care towards Longnor, and 400m later turn left just before the bend to gain the High Peak Trail (HPT, marked as Pennine Bridleway on many maps) at **Sparklow**. Turn right to go northwards along the trail for 2km to reach its end, then turn left onto a stony track (following R68).

Turn right at a T-junction after 800m, reaching a second T-junction some 800m later.

Fantastic **views** over Hitter, Parkhurst and Chrome Hills can be seen from a high point on the road just before Wheeldon Trees.

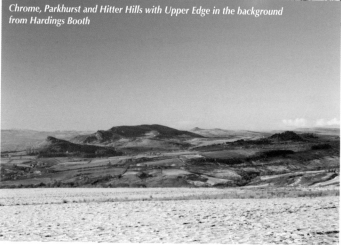

Chrome, Parkhurst and Hitter Hills with Upper Edge in the background from Hardings Booth

Turn right again and continue for 1.3km to reach another junction just south of **Earl Sterndale**. Fork right and continue through the centre of the village past The Quiet Woman PH to eventually reach a crossroads.

It is hoped that a new extension to the HPT will be developed within the lifetime of this guidebook; however, shortly before going to press we heard that it was not going to be developed as early as planned. But please keep an eye on the updates section of the Cicerone website for more information on this as it progresses.

Turn right at the cross-roads and along the B5053. Continue for 2.6km over a long hill and past an entrance to the huge **Hill Head Quarry**, to reach a junction just beyond the **Brierlow Bar** bookshop and before the A515. Turn left here and continue for 2.6 km into **Harpur Hill**. Bear right at a junction by the **church** and descend for 1km to reach the busy **A515** on the outskirts of **Buxton**. Turn left onto this; rise steeply uphill initially, then descend gently to a major crossroads. Go straight ahead, rising gently through the market place before descending to reach a major roundabout with the A53. Turn right to return to the **station**.

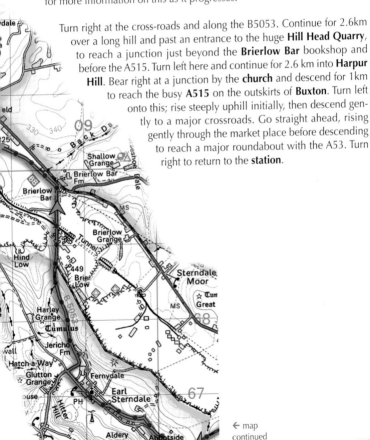

← map
continued
from p122

125

ROUTE 16

GRINDLEFORD LOOP VIA EDALE

Distance	59km
Total ascent/descent	1291m
Grade	Hard
Surface	81% road, 2% trail, 17% off-road
Start/finish	Grindleford rail station SK 254 788
Parking	Free parking is available on the access road to the rail station, but be careful not to use spaces immediately next to café, as they are private
Cycle hire	Nearest is at Hassop Station on the Monsal Trail, SK 218 705
Road bikes?	Not recommended

Hilly but varied route, with plenty of escape options and ancient plague village of Eyam. Final section is lovely lumpy off-road which isn't overly hard.

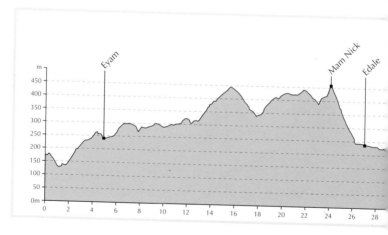

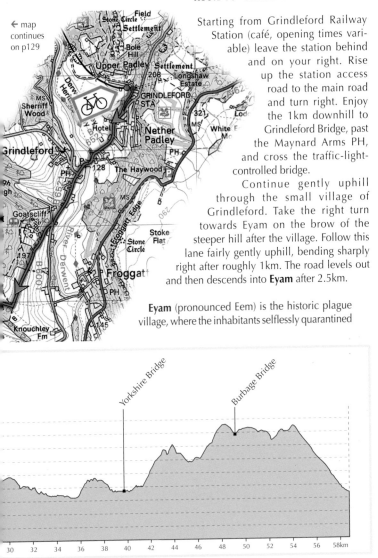

← map continues on p129

Starting from Grindleford Railway Station (café, opening times variable) leave the station behind and on your right. Rise up the station access road to the main road and turn right. Enjoy the 1km downhill to Grindleford Bridge, past the Maynard Arms PH, and cross the traffic-light-controlled bridge.

Continue gently uphill through the small village of Grindleford. Take the right turn towards Eyam on the brow of the steeper hill after the village. Follow this lane fairly gently uphill, bending sharply right after roughly 1km. The road levels out and then descends into **Eyam** after 2.5km.

Eyam (pronounced Eem) is the historic plague village, where the inhabitants selflessly quarantined

127

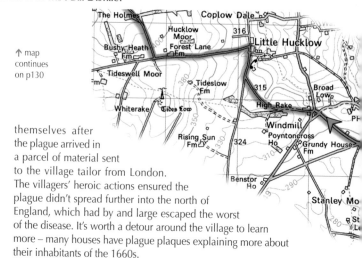

↑ map
continues
on p130

themselves after
the plague arrived in
a parcel of material sent
to the village tailor from London.
The villagers' heroic actions ensured the
plague didn't spread further into the north of
England, which had by and large escaped the worst
of the disease. It's worth a detour around the village to learn
more – many houses have plague plaques explaining more about
their inhabitants of the 1660s.

Arriving at the triangular 'Square', where there are a couple of tea shops, bear right up Church Street. Follow this past the primary school and Eyam Hall (tea shop inside). The road bears right and then left, then gently climbs to reach a turn to Tideswell Lane.

Looking back along Tideswell Lane, Eyam

On this corner there's an interesting house which used to keep **carrier pigeons** to communicate with the silk mills in Macclesfield.

Turn sharp left up this lane, and continue straight ahead where Windmill Lane branches off left. The tarmac ends at Fairview Farm 150m later, and the route now continues on a lovely stone

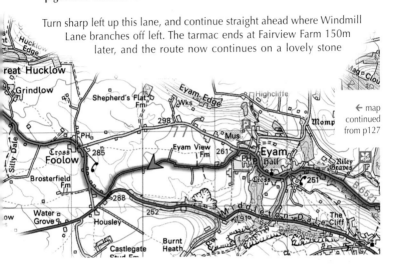

← map continued from p127

track. Ignore farm tracks either side, and continue straight ahead for 1.8km, with bends and a dip to cross Linen Dale 300m before the end of the track.

At the end of the track, turn right at a T-junction with a country lane, close to a junction with A623. Continue straight ahead for 800m into Foolow village to reach a T-junction opposite The Bulls Head PH.

Foolow village is a pretty stone-built village based around a traditional village green with 14th-century cross and duckpond.

Turn left here and continue past the green out of the village towards Great Hucklow for 1.8km. You will cross over one intermediate lane after about 1.3km, and another about 500m later. Very soon after this you cross the B6049 with an awkward left–right dog-leg, to enter the tiny village of **Windmill**.

Continue through the village for 1.2km and turn right at the T-junction at the end. After 400m ignore a turn right to **Little Hucklow** in a dip, and continue uphill to Hill Top Farm. Turn left towards Peak Forest opposite this, and continue for 1.3km, passing Forest Lane Farm. About 200m beyond the farm, turn right onto a stony track (250m before Bushy Heath Farm Campsite). Continue

→ map
continued
on p1

↑ map
continued
from p128

up this easy track for 1.1km, to join a country lane at a bend. Turn right to continue straight ahead and shortly afterwards the road bends right and soon heads downhill.

Enjoy a welcome descent through old mine workings down to a T-junction. Turn left here and bear left again past the turning to the cement works. The road ahead has been progressively diverted over the years into a great semicircle, to skirt an ever encroaching quarry, and now curves right.

As the road starts to descend, bear left onto a short dirt track which passes through a gateway to join a track at the top of **Dirtlow Rake**.

> Technically speaking the **rights of way** over this short section off the track linking Dirtlow Rake to the road are not clear. In practice it is well-used by riders and it is unlikely that you will encounter problems using it, but if challenged be prepared to continue 1km further down the country lane to gain access to the bottom of Dirtlow Rake. Turn left onto the rough track and walk back up (or ride it if you can!).

Turn left, reaching plateau level again and passing a well-restored quarry with good views across to Mam Tor. After about 800m you pass through a gate to cross the Limestone Way at a junction of walls. Bear right 200m later at a gate to stay on the main track. Continue gently uphill, through a further gate, and past Rowter Farm to reach the road 1.4km later.

Turn right down the road, passing right turns for Castleton and Blue John Cavern. Take care to safely negotiate the severe left bend at the latter junction. The road now climbs past woodland, which hides your sharp right turn towards Edale. There's a short steep climb up to Mam Nick, before a well-earned and fantastic lengthy descent to **Barber Booth**, losing 240m of height over 2km. The next 10km follows the road along the Edale Valley, undulating slightly but roughly paralleling the railway to reach **Hope** and a couple of good tea shops.

> **Edale** is actually a conglomeration of five 'booths' or ancient farm settlements based around Grindsbrook Booth (where the main village is now). When the railway station opened, the name of Edale began to be used for the collection of villages rather than the dale itself.

In Hope, turn left onto the busy main road towards Hathersage for 350m, before turning left into a side-road towards Aston (only). Follow this uphill, ignoring a steep upward side-turn left after about

1km. In **Aston**, ignore Parsons Lane on the right, instead following the 'unsuitable for motors' road straight ahead.

Continue along for 1.3km past Ryecroft Cottage Farm, and gently down to the end of Carr Lane in **Thornhill** village. Here, turn left at the T-junction towards Ladybower. When you reach a parking area on the right, you have a choice of routes.

On the left, opposite the parking area, a new bridleway (Thornhill Trail) gently climbs for 1.2km along the valley side, where it joins a steeper tarmac track (concessionary bridleway) leading to the end of the Ladybower dam wall. Here you will need to dismount and walk along the footpath over the dam wall to reach the A6013 (Ashopton Road). Turn right along it past the **Yorkshire Bridge** Inn, and turn left up New Road after about 500m.

Whichever way you get there, New Road gives you a long slow grind uphill to plateau level on a country lane with a welcome shady canopy. Eventually the gradient eases, and the lane undulates

→ map continued from p130

Looking back down the hill towards Stanage Plantation under Stanage Edge

gently around the height of Bamford Edge.

You reach a T-junction at the foot of a moderately steep descent after about 2.5km. Turn left, and continue along for 300m past Dennis Knoll (pine plantation), passing over a cattle grid into North Lees Estate. Ignore the tough bridleway ahead, and instead follow the tarmac right, gently descending and then re-ascending, passing Stanage Plantation car park (mobile coffee shop with very good proper coffee, ☎ 07788 137462). Soon afterwards turn left at a T-junction and rise moderately uphill to pass Hooks Car car park.

Turn left at this T-junction and continue fairly gently uphill for 1km back to the plateau of **Burbage Moor**. As you round a bend left, the gradient eases, and the views open out significantly across the Burbage Valley, with Higgar Tor being very prominent. After about 1.2km, give way to a road which merges from the right.

Continue for a further 2.4km passing the bends at Upper Burbage Bridge. The road gently climbs, and as you start to descend, watch out for a white gate to nowhere on the left. This marks the place where a track branches off to the right. Take this lovely dirt track gently downhill for just over 1km to reach Houndkirk Road at a moorland crossing of trails.

→ map continues on p134

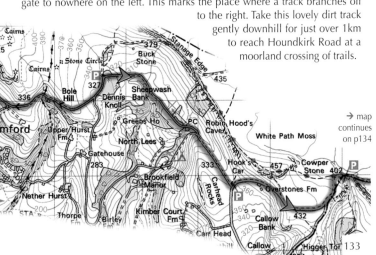

This used to be an ancient **packhorse toll road**, and is now a fantastic off-road trail that's almost mountain biking territory in a few places, but just gentle enough to be included here!

Turn right and follow Houndkirk Road for 3km, gently rising then falling over **Houndkirk Moor**. The final descent brings you to a gate next to the drive to Parson House, and shortly afterwards you reach the A6187. Turn right down the main road, bending right past the Fox House Inn, and take the second left – signposted towards Grindleford. Continue down this road, being careful not to miss the sharp right turn into **Grindleford** station in 2.6km.

→ map continued from p133

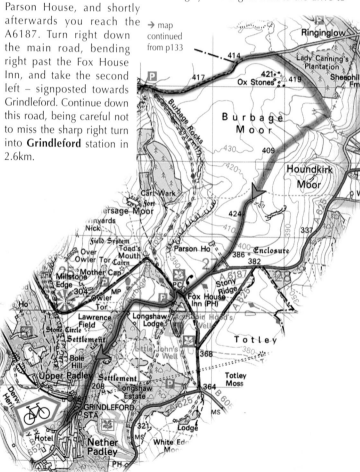

ROUTE 17

BAMFORD LOOP VIA MAM TOR

Distance	41 km
Total ascent/descent	965m
Grade	Hard
Surface	70% road, 30% off-road
Start/finish	Bamford railway station car park SK 207 825
Parking	Limited free parking in station car park, behind Sheffield-bound platform
Cycle hire	Available from Peak Cycle Hire (Fairholmes)
Road bikes?	Not recommended

Surprisingly the real killer hill isn't Mam Tor but a smaller additional hill at Dam Dale that can be avoided if required!

From Bamford Railway Station car park head up the access road, turning sharp left at the end onto the A6013. Cross over the railway bridge and continue down to the traffic lights at the junction with A6187.

Turn right, the road soon crosses a river bridge and passes a garden centre. Take a narrow lane left opposite it to **Shatton**. Ignore all side-roads in the village until you reach a small ford on a

← map continues on p137

Crossing very dry ford (in summer) at the end of Shatton Village

slight turn right (roughly 500m). Cross this, and head gently uphill for 800m, to reach the gateway into Shatton Hall Farm.

Turn right and away from the farm, through a wide wooden gate, and continue up a stony vehicle track passing a blue gate on your left. Continue straight ahead then downhill, passing through three gates, to reach a country lane (Brough Lane) on a sharp bend. Turn right and continue downhill for roughly 300m to reach **Brough** village.

Turn left onto a main road, and cross a narrow bridge by the old Vincent Works. Continue into **Bradwell** village (roughly 1.3km). About 300m beyond an inn, bear right up a lane alongside the village green and playground.

At the top of the green, ignore Michlow Drive, and take a public bridleway to the right shortly afterwards. Follow this rough tarmac lane, ignoring a footpath to the left and head uphill for roughly 400m. At the crest, turn right onto a narrower, but initially better surfaced track to the right of a gateway.

Go through a metal gateway, and bear gently left just past a white-topped limestone gatepost, following blue arrows on a wider stony track which snakes down a steep dip. Beware of a short gravel trap at the bottom. Cross the works road

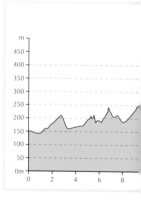

136

with care (especially if mid-week) and up the path on the far side. Try not to stop at the start of this path – it can be hard to get restarted!

The bridleway passes under three enclosed conveyor bridges and across a second works road to join a dirt path running through woodland. After roughly 400m, the trail divides rather artificially alongside a cottage. Take the left fork which immediately joins a stony vehicle track, and reaches a tarmac country lane on a sharp bend. Join this, heading straight ahead and briefly uphill. Soon a gentle downhill leads to an

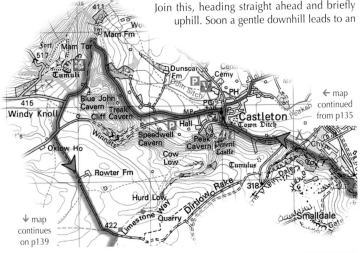

← map continued from p135

↓ map continues on p139

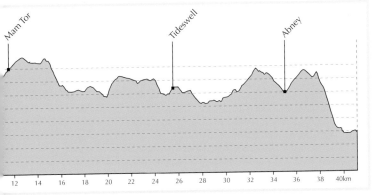

Looking back down the old (broken) Mam Tor road

acute T-junction. Turn right and further downhill to reach **Castleton**'s village green and war memorial.

From the green, head downhill past the front of the YHA and The George PH to reach the main street through Castleton. Turn left along here, descending slightly to a roundabout (and café). Continue over the roundabout and climb gently for about 600m until you pass a junction where vehicle traffic turns left to Chapel-en-le-Frith. Keep straight ahead on the old main road. Climb gently up this, past Speedwell Cavern Coach Park, and Treak Cliff Cavern.

Where you reach the end of public vehicle access, it may be worth a brief detour left to see Odin Mine, the oldest named mine in Derbyshire.

Now start the steeper climb up the (disused) Mam Tor road, still on good tarmac for another 500m or so. Go through a wooden gate to climb up the broken section of road, which has a few awkward sections that may well require a dismount.

The **Mam Tor road** used to be one of the main roads connecting Sheffield and Manchester before 1979, when the local highways authority gave up trying to maintain a road built over weak shale bedrock, as it was in a permanent state of shuffling down the mountain.

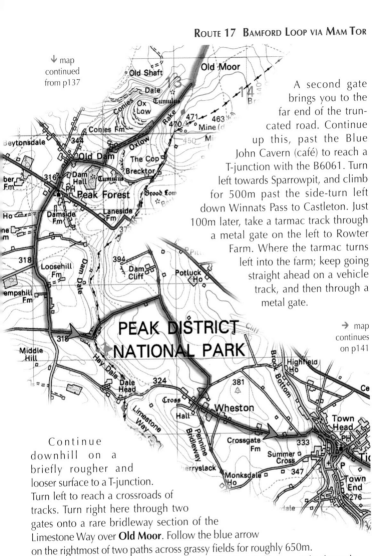

↓ map
continued
from p137

A second gate brings you to the far end of the truncated road. Continue up this, past the Blue John Cavern (café) to reach a T-junction with the B6061. Turn left towards Sparrowpit, and climb for 500m past the side-turn left down Winnats Pass to Castleton. Just 100m later, take a tarmac track through a metal gate on the left to Rowter Farm. Where the tarmac turns left into the farm; keep going straight ahead on a vehicle track, and then through a metal gate.

→ map
continues
on p141

Continue downhill on a briefly rougher and looser surface to a T-junction. Turn left to reach a crossroads of tracks. Turn right here through two gates onto a rare bridleway section of the Limestone Way over **Old Moor**. Follow the blue arrow on the rightmost of two paths across grassy fields for roughly 650m. At a junction of paths in the far corner of the first field, turn right through a wooden gateway. A farm-track joins from the right, continue downhill onto a rougher track (along Oxlow Rake) with a gateway at each end of the rough section: the gradient eases after this.

At the foot of the descent, turn left onto a tarmac drive. Shortly after, turn right and descend to Old Dam (part of **Peak Forest** village). Turn left at the island, and continue for roughly 500m. Take a dog-leg right then left at traffic lights across the A623 towards Smalldale. Continue for roughly 1km, passing a donkey village, then where the main road bends right, go straight ahead towards Wheston.

If conditions are reasonably dry, turn left onto the Pennine Bridleway (PBW) in roughly 1km, opposite the side-road to Smalldale. The surface is rough but generally solid down into Hay Dale. Turn sharply left along a looser surface to continue up and out of Dam Dale on the PBW. As the gradient steepens, the surface increases in roughness but gets more solid. In roughly 400m the gradient, and then surface, eases significantly. The remaining 600m is much easier going to reach a tarmac country lane. Turn right and downhill on this, ignoring a track joining from the left after roughly 1.4km, arriving at the tiny hamlet of **Wheston** soon afterwards. Turn left and uphill at the T-junction.

> To **avoid this challenge** (it's physically tougher uphill than the Mam Tor road, although not as technical) continue a further 300m past the PBW and take the next tarmac lane left. Follow this for roughly 2km to reach Wheston.

Continue uphill out of Wheston towards Tideswell. After roughly 1.8km, turn right at a T-junction at the foot of a steep descent into **Tideswell**. Bend right

Stopping to admire the view from Shatton Moor

and pass the Star Inn PH to reach the village centre opposite the Natwest Bank. Turn left to pass Tindalls Bakery and the 'Cathedral of the Peak' (or detour right for a tea shop).

Pass the George Hotel, and 50m later turn sharply right up Church Lane (The Cliffe). The steep gradient soon eases and eventually begins a gentle descent into **Litton**. Turn left at the T-junction outside the Red Lion PH. This road is initially uphill, then gives a long downhill with wide views to join the A623. Turn left onto this

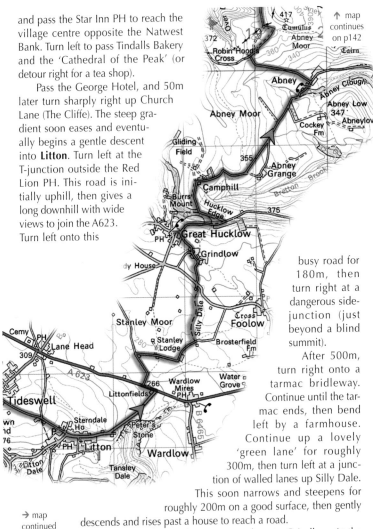

↑ map continues on p142

→ map continued from p139

busy road for 180m, then turn right at a dangerous side-junction (just beyond a blind summit).

After 500m, turn right onto a tarmac bridleway. Continue until the tarmac ends, then bend left by a farmhouse. Continue up a lovely 'green lane' for roughly 300m, then turn left at a junction of walled lanes up Silly Dale. This soon narrows and steepens for roughly 200m on a good surface, then gently descends and rises past a house to reach a road.

Cross over this, and up a narrow lane to Grindlow. At the top of the hill, follow the tarmac leftwards, and ignore a left turn

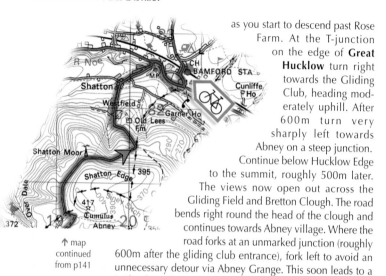

↑ map
continued
from p141

as you start to descend past Rose Farm. At the T-junction on the edge of **Great Hucklow** turn right towards the Gliding Club, heading moderately uphill. After 600m turn very sharply left towards Abney on a steep junction. Continue below Hucklow Edge to the summit, roughly 500m later. The views now open out across the Gliding Field and Bretton Clough. The road bends right round the head of the clough and continues towards Abney village. Where the road forks at an unmarked junction (roughly 600m after the gliding club entrance), fork left to avoid an unnecessary detour via Abney Grange. This soon leads to a 1.5km long descent into **Abney**.

Look out carefully here for a very easily-missed red phone box on the right (almost behind a farm building). Directly opposite the phone box, take a tarmac track left towards Robin Hood's Cross. Climb rough tarmac for about 800m; pass through a gate at its end, and turn right towards Shatton on a stony track (restricted byway). Your track bends left where a footpath branches off right, then soon bends right through a gate. Head clockwise around Shatton Edge and pass the radio transmitter on **Shatton Moor**.

Soon after the transmitter start descending carefully, on a fairly solid but gravel-ridden track (loose in places). When rough tarmac is regained on a bend left, beware of a couple of speed-bumps at the top and loose gravel and sharp bends on the steep descent, to emerge just above the ford at **Shatton**.

Turn right, and follow the road through Shatton to the A6187, being careful of the narrow bridge at the end of Shatton. Turn right onto the main road, then sneak left on the cycle lane that begins at the traffic lights, over the rail bridge and right to return to Bamford Station car park.

ROUTE 18

MIDDLEWOOD LOOP VIA PYM CHAIR

Distance	37km
Total ascent/descent	900m
Grade	Hard
Surface	68% road, 32% trail
Start/Finish	Middlewood Station (by rail) SJ 945 848/Nelson's Pit visitor centre (by car) SJ 945 834
Getting to the start/ parking/cycle hire	As Route 4
Road bikes?	Reasonable

A very hilly route with awesome views over the Kettleshulme valley.

↑ map continues on p144

From the visitor centre car park exit past the height limiting barrier. Cross the road and descend the steps to reach the Middlewood Way, initially running on the old platform. Turn right and continue north, heading under bridge 15. Continue past bridges 16–18 and the footpath to station/turnoff to Jackson's Brickworks, to pass above Middlewood Station about 1.5km from the visitor centre.

From Middlewood Station, head up steps/ramp from the station platform to the bridge. Turn right (north) along the Middlewood Way.

After the station, continue along the trail; after 2.5km the gravel gives way to tarmac all the way into **Marple**. The tarmac trail crosses a minor road/car park with A-bars, and then continues for a final

143

View across Goyt Valley and Macclesfield Canal from Marple Ridge End

↑ map
continued
from p143

450m to end at A-bars on a road opposite Marple Allotments. Bear right onto the road and continue past Rose Hill Station (Marple) to reach a junction with the busy A626.

Turn right onto the main road, using the toucan crossing to the right if necessary towards the town centre. Turn right at the first set of traffic lights (by petrol station) up Church Lane. Continue up this one-way street past the Hatters Arms to reach a mini roundabout. Cross this, and continue straight ahead (two-way now) past the Pineapple PH.

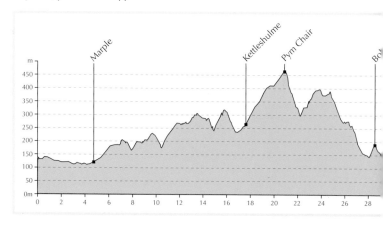

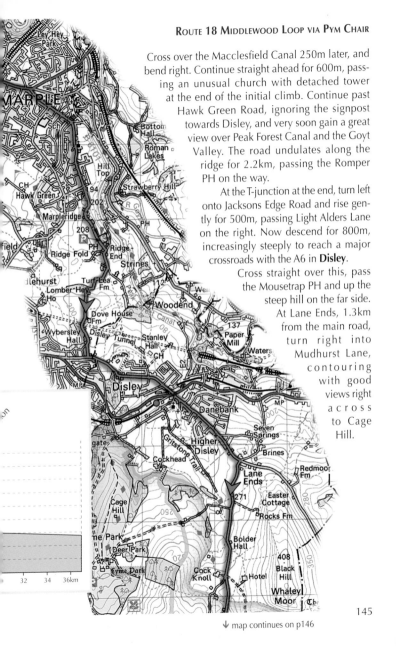

Cross over the Macclesfield Canal 250m later, and bend right. Continue straight ahead for 600m, passing an unusual church with detached tower at the end of the initial climb. Continue past Hawk Green Road, ignoring the signpost towards Disley, and very soon gain a great view over Peak Forest Canal and the Goyt Valley. The road undulates along the ridge for 2.2km, passing the Romper PH on the way.

At the T-junction at the end, turn left onto Jacksons Edge Road and rise gently for 500m, passing Light Alders Lane on the right. Now descend for 800m, increasingly steeply to reach a major crossroads with the A6 in **Disley**.

Cross straight over this, pass the Mousetrap PH and up the steep hill on the far side. At Lane Ends, 1.3km from the main road, turn right into Mudhurst Lane, contouring with good views right across to Cage Hill.

145

↓ map continues on p146

↓ map
continued
from p145

← map
continues
on p148

View over Windgather Rocks

The Cage was built in the early 18th century by the Legh family as a **hunting lodge** with outstanding views over the grounds. Today it is owned by the National Trust (part of Lyme Park).

Rise up moderately for 1.6km, passing Bolder Hall Farm then Moorside Grange Hotel. Over the next 3.1km, the road descends to a narrow bridge and then climbs past Higher Cliff Farm (and a layby with a fantastic view over the Todd Brook Valley below). From the summit soon beyond, descend quite steeply to a T-junction with a more major road.

Turn left down the B5470 for a further 1 km, descending to a bridge over the Todd Brook with a short steep rise beyond. The gradient soon eases to bring you into **Kettleshulme**.

Just before the primary school, turn right towards Saltersford and continue moderately uphill, passing Side End Farm to reach a crossroads after 1.1km. Cross this and grind gently uphill for roughly 700m underneath **Windgather Rocks**. Then, as the gradient eases, continue for a further 1.3km along the ridgeline to reach a high junction near Pym Chair (**Oldgate Nick**).

Turn right and descend a very steep, narrow and twisting hill. Stay on the main road as it bends left at **Jenkin Chapel** and descends further before re-ascending to a T-junction at Nab End. Turn right onto Ewrin Lane, continuing steeply uphill on a 'holloway'.

Holloways are ancient sunken roads. Usually the height of the ground around them indicates that the road has sunk from its original level during the days of horse and cart. These compacted the often muddy surface of pre-motorised vehicle unsealed roads. This one has an additional clue to its ancient origin – a memorial to the mystery of John Turner's death in 1755.

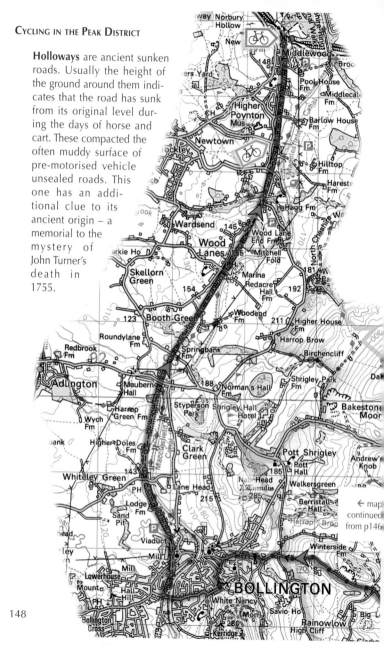

← map continued from p146

After Buxter Stoops Farm, the lane gently undulates across high meadowland. Continue straight ahead past a side turn left to Rainow, and it's just one last gentle rise to Pike Low before descending towards Bollington.

This road ends at a staggered crossroads opposite Four Lane Ends Farm. Turn right then left to continue descending steeply to Bollington on a country lane carrying the Cheshire Cycleway. This descent continues for 2.6km past the Poachers PH to reach a T-junction at the edge of **Bollington** by the New Con Club PH on Ingersley Road. Turn left to gain a roundabout, and straight over onto Palmerston Street.

Descend gently for 200m, and as the road bends right and downhill, turn left into the narrow High Street, just before a car park entrance on the right. Descend gently initially, then rise up steeply to a T-junction by the Red Lion PH. Turn right here and continue along to a junction with Jackson and Grimshaw Lanes. Turn right on Grimshaw Lane and continue along this for 550m. Descend under a traffic-light-controlled bridge under the canal, and 100m later, turn right onto the Middlewood Way opposite Clough Bank road.

Continue up this easy-going trail to return to the start (6.6km for the car park or 7.7km for the rail station), soon crossing the fine viaduct across Bollington town.

Jenkin Chapel, Cheshire

ROUTE 19

MARSDEN LOOP VIA SADDLEWORTH MOOR	
Distance	48km
Total ascent/descent	1425m
Grade	Hard
Surface	87% road, 13% off-road
Direction	Best done clockwise (as described) to keep time on the busy A road to a minimum
Start/finish	Marsden railway station SE 047 119
Parking	Limited parking is available on the streets nearby: station car park for rail users only
Cycle hire	Wheelie Fun in Hebden Bridge
Road bikes?	Not recommended

Some big hills and A road riding make this a challenging route, but the views are worth the effort.

Head downhill from Marsden railway station on Station Road, past the Health Centre and bending right over the river to continue up the main shopping street. Cross over the A62 into Peel Street, passing a park with a bandstand on the left, then turn left at the top of the road.

Continue for 500m to the end of Carrs Road and bear right onto Meltham Road following R68 fairly steeply uphill to pass Hill Farm, where the going becomes a lot easier. There are good views across the Colne Valley here.

Bend past the White House PH and descend for 500m into a narrow and twisting section at Holt Head. Here, turn left towards Slaithwaite along Varley Road, and then immediately right onto Holt End Road. This undulates for 2km into **Blackmoorfoot**.

Pass the Bulls Head PH then climb gently for 200m to reach a side-turning right beside a bus turning circle. Take this steeply uphill for 200m, then turn right onto Reservoir Side Road, passing an old quarry on the left. Beyond the houses at the end, the road becomes a pleasant bridleway, with occasional deep sand, giving a gentle descent over 500m to reach a country lane.

Turn right down the narrowing lane, and into a small hamlet (**Crosland Edge**). Bend right down Harrison Lane and at its bottom turn left onto Helme Lane and into **Meltham**.

After 800m turn left into Broadlands Road, now following R68 again. Turn right at the end; 150m later turn bear left onto Station Street and past Morrison's supermarket. Continue uphill to reach a crossroads with the B6108 by The Swan PH. Turn right towards Greenfield on Wessenden Head Road and start the 2.9km long grinding climb up **Meltham Moor** to the road summit at 465m altitude, re-entering the national park after 1.1km and crossing a cattle grid.

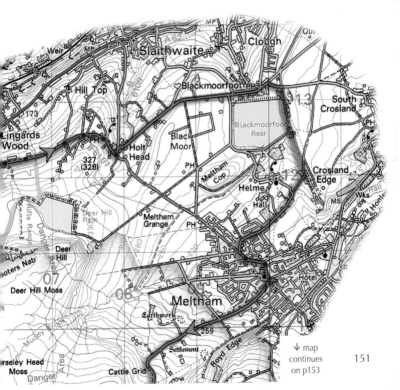

↓ map
continues
on p153

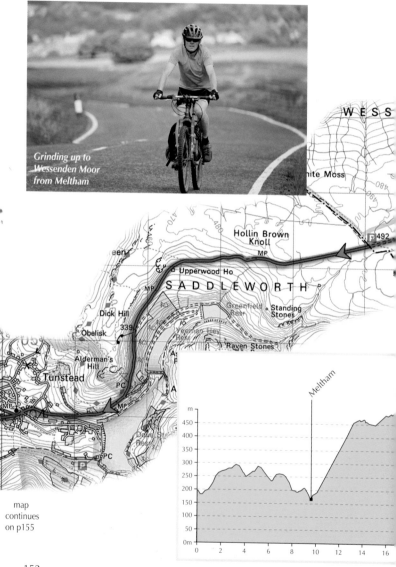

Grinding up to
Wessenden Moor
from Meltham

map
continues
on p155

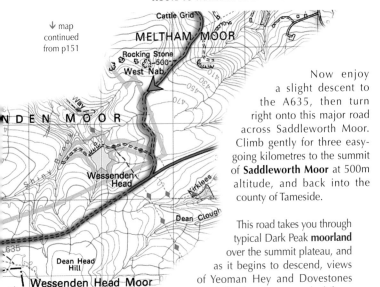

↓ map
continued
from p151

Now enjoy a slight descent to the A635, then turn right onto this major road across Saddleworth Moor. Climb gently for three easy-going kilometres to the summit of **Saddleworth Moor** at 500m altitude, and back into the county of Tameside.

This road takes you through typical Dark Peak **moorland** over the summit plateau, and as it begins to descend, views of Yeoman Hey and Dovestones Reservoirs begin to appear on the left.

Enjoy 6km of fast descent past the reservoirs into **Tunstead**, to reach a roundabout by the Clarence PH.

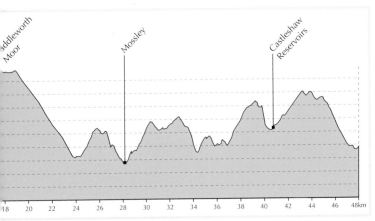

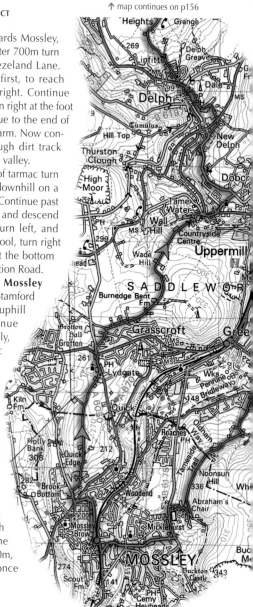

↑ map continues on p156

Take the left fork towards Mossley, passing a school (right). After 700m turn left onto the PBW up Friezeland Lane. This rises up, steeply at first, to reach Greenmans Lane on the right. Continue past this, and 70m later turn right at the foot of Intake Lane and continue to the end of the tarmac by Noon Sun Farm. Now contour the hillside on a rough dirt track with great views across the valley.

At a brief resumption of tarmac turn right at a T-junction, and downhill on a deteriorated tarmac track. Continue past the water treatment plant, and descend onto the B6175 below. Turn left, and 100m later, opposite a school, turn right down Winterford Road. At the bottom bend left as it becomes Station Road.

Immediately before **Mossley** rail station, turn left onto Stamford Road, bending right and uphill over the railway. Continue uphill for 500m, fairly steeply, with glimpses of fantastic views over the valley to the right. Bend left as the gradient eases, and reach a traffic-light-controlled junction with the A670.

Cross this rightwards onto Lees Road, then take the third right up Quickedge Road. This gives a steep climb and fine views, passing Seville's Buildings and Little Haigh Farm. After the summit the surface deteriorates for 200m, but soon regains tarmac once more. Continue straight ahead, descending and climbing again to gain a more major road close to **Lydgate** Church.

Continue past the White Hart PH and through traffic calming to reach a crossroads. Go over the A669 here into Platting Road. After 100m, fork right onto Burnedge Lane, and continue straight ahead for roughly 1.2km to reach the road summit by Lower Bent Farm.

Descend, on an increasingly steep road, to a hazardous junction where three roads come together. Turn right along Delph New Road, then bend left over a river bridge. Bear left at the Shambles PH towards Dobcross up Woods Lane.

The houses on this road are quite an unusual mix of traditional and very contemporary takes on the typical Yorkshire stone-built house, and **Dobcross** is clearly proud of its 19th-century trading history – how many villages of this size would have had their own bank in the village square? This bank was undoubtedly aided by the growth of the Platt Brothers' pioneering cotton spinning machine business – they grew to be the largest global manufacturer of textile machinery in the 19th-century world.

In **Dobcross** village square, turn left onto Platt Lane; after a brief rise, this narrow lane descends towards the bridge at New Delph. Don't go too fast or you'll miss a turning as the road bends left just 80m before it ends at the bridge. Turn right onto this (Midgrove Lane), then after 200m, cross the A62 into Rumbles Lane. Continue along this narrow country lane until it reaches Hill End Road. Turn left along this and continue enjoying the quiet back roads of **Delph** for a total of 600m.

Emerging by the White Lion PH, go straight ahead onto the main road. Opposite a school on the left, turn right into Friarmere Road. Turn left at the end onto Springwood Way, and continue straight ahead up Lodge Lane where Springwood Way forks right.

← map
continued
from p152

Continue steeply uphill for 700m past Edge Hill, and roughly 250m later continue straight ahead on Broad Lane at a junction with Heights Lane. Continue past the imposing hill-top church and Royal Oak PH for 900m, crossing over a junction before the tarmac ends by a large new house. Bear slightly left here along a rough (rutted) continuation bridle-way which rises and then descends to a crossroads of tracks after 900m. Turn right through a gate and descend steeply and roughly (stony) for 450m to **Castleshaw Reservoirs** on the PBW.

On the track above Castleshaw Reservoirs

At the bottom, turn left through a gate beside the reservoir onto a much smoother surfaced track, then right across the dam wall (Castleshaw Top Bank). Bend left at the end and gently uphill on a twisty lane passing Bleak Hey Nook to emerge on Standedge Foot Road.

Turn left to remain on the PBW, rising moderately steeply for roughly 1km to reach Rock Farm at the end of the tarmac. To escape the rough section ahead, turn right down Manor Lane to join the main road.

Continue up the wide rough track for 500m to its summit; shortly after this follow the PBW where it turns off right to cross the A62. Continue briefly down the track ahead for 100m, then follow a signpost for Standedge Car Park left, up a short steep bank to a gate at the top. Pass through the gate and along beside a small reservoir to arrive at **Standedge** Car Park.

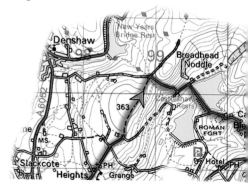

↑ map
continued
from p154

The next section contains an off-road section (which is in the process of becoming part of a new bridleway link into the Pennine Bridleway) which crosses a council boundary. Oldham Council are happy it is now a bridleway but Kirklees Council (who cover the part after the stile) insist it is still legally a footpath. However, the landowner (National Trust) believes it is already a bridleway and has no issues with responsible cyclists riding across it, so you shouldn't encounter any issues. But as always, if challenged, be polite, state the situation calmly and non-confrontationally, but be prepared to dismount or even deviate if need be.

The deviation goes left and over the road summit of Standedge along a particularly dangerous part of the A62 over to Standedge Car Park before taking 1st right into Mount Road just before The Carriage House. If forced to use this, prudent cyclists would dismount and walk as far from the road edge as possible!

From the right hand side of the car park, a new part of PBW link track climbs the cutting side, paralleling the A62 now far below, for about 300m until a gate is reached. Pass through the gate, and follow the obvious track, descending gradually past **Redbrook Reservoir** and coming slowly closer to the road on the left. The road is eventually reached by a well surfaced track which turns sharply away to the left, crossing the intervening gully.

Turn right down Mount road, and at the bottom, cross over the roundabout onto Carrs Road. Continue for 250m to reach your outward route by the small park with a bandstand. Turn left down this road (Peel Street) and retrace your steps, following signs to Marsden railway station.

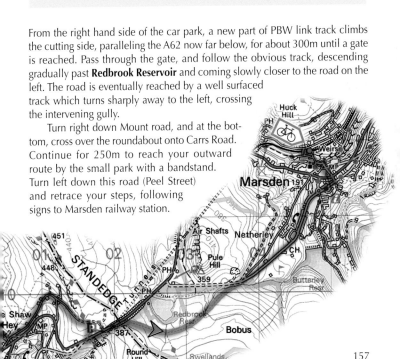

ROUTE 20

MACCLESFIELD LOOP VIA THE ROACHES

Distance	51km
Total ascent/descent	1225m
Grade	Hard
Surface	100% road
Start/Finish	Macclesfield railway station SJ 919 736
Parking	Opposite Macclesfield railway station on Waters Green by the Old Millstone Inn
Cycle Hire	Nearest available is Peak Tours (Glossop) or Longdendale Valley (Hadfield)
Road bikes?	Good

A hilly route from Macclesfield into the Peak District and over the Roaches, taking in several lovely quiet lanes.

Leaving Macclesfield railway station behind you, turn left along Sunderland Street. Go straight ahead through two sets of traffic lights, and immediately before the third, turn left beside the park onto Park Green following R55.

Continue to the end of this cobbled road, crossing a small footbridge over a stream with bollards either side.

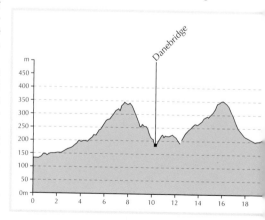

Turn right onto the road beyond and go straight across into Waterside at the junction under the flyover. The road steepens up at the end, turn left over the railway bridge on Windmill Street, then right into Calamine

Street, which soon becomes Heapy Street. Continue along this to a T-junction with Gunco Lane.

Turn right onto this road and continue to the end, turning left at the T-junction by the Railway View PH onto Byrons Lane. Ignoring a fork right, continue past the Old Kings Head PH and under the canal aqueduct. Where a side-road forks left some 200m after the aqueduct, continue ahead (following signs towards Wincle for the next 4km).

Continue straight ahead through **Sutton** village

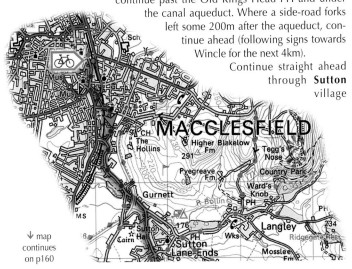

↓ map
continues
on p160

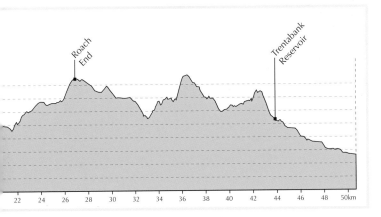

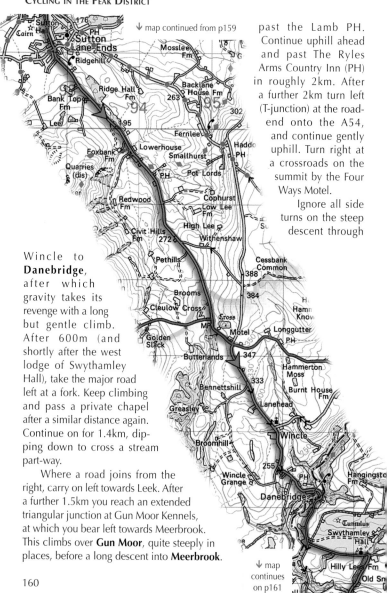

↓ map continued from p159

past the Lamb PH. Continue uphill ahead and past The Ryles Arms Country Inn (PH) in roughly 2km. After a further 2km turn left (T-junction) at the road-end onto the A54, and continue gently uphill. Turn right at a crossroads on the summit by the Four Ways Motel.

Ignore all side turns on the steep descent through

Wincle to **Danebridge**, after which gravity takes its revenge with a long but gentle climb. After 600m (and shortly after the west lodge of Swythamley Hall), take the major road left at a fork. Keep climbing and pass a private chapel after a similar distance again. Continue on for 1.4km, dipping down to cross a stream part-way.

Where a road joins from the right, carry on left towards Leek. After a further 1.5km you reach an extended triangular junction at Gun Moor Kennels, at which you bear left towards Meerbrook. This climbs over **Gun Moor**, quite steeply in places, before a long descent into **Meerbrook**.

↓ map continues on p161

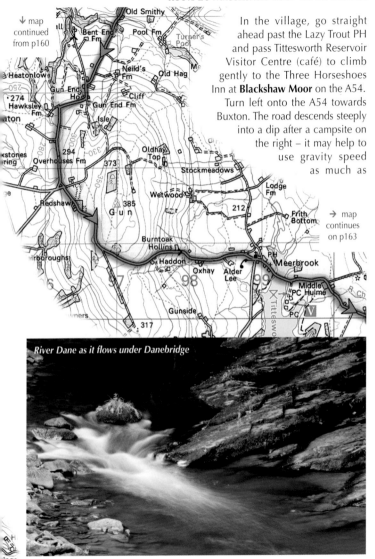

In the village, go straight ahead past the Lazy Trout PH and pass Tittesworth Reservoir Visitor Centre (café) to climb gently to the Three Horseshoes Inn at **Blackshaw Moor** on the A54. Turn left onto the A54 towards Buxton. The road descends steeply into a dip after a campsite on the right – it may help to use gravity speed as much as

→ map continues on p163

↓ map continued from p160

River Dane as it flows under Danebridge

Tittesworth Reservoir in the distance with rosebay willowherb in the foreground

possible to save effort on the steep pull out of the dip on the far side. Fortunately it is not too far up the hill before you reach a side-turn left towards Upper Hulme.

Take this, continuing uphill at first, but soon turn left and downhill, following signs for a tea room, to a stream crossing in **Upper Hulme**. Continue round the sharp bend and through the old mill buildings, and moderately gently uphill.

Continue past The Roaches tea room, 1.5km from Upper Hulme and continue a further 1.6km over deteriorating tarmac past a side-turn left to Meerbrook. Continue ahead towards Royal Cottage, up an increasingly steep gorse-lined hill. Pass through a gate (sometimes open) in 460m and continue a further 400m to the cattle grid at **Roach End**. (An ice cream van is often found here in good weather.)

Continue on the road uphill and around the bend right, to gain the road summit on the far side of the hill in roughly 400m. The gentle descent downhill is surprisingly fast: take care with the bends and cattle grids. Continue down to a stream, before rising moderately steeply uphill past a side-turn right. Continue past Hazel Barrow kennels for a further 225m to a triangular junction (occasional café) and turn left.

The road initially descends gently, before levelling out past two side turns right. It then leads to a final steep winding descent over a narrow bridge to a T-junction. Turn left and downhill towards Gradbach.

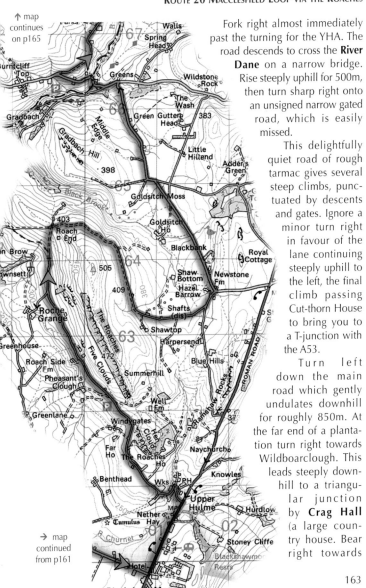

Fork right almost immediately past the turning for the YHA. The road descends to cross the **River Dane** on a narrow bridge. Rise steeply uphill for 500m, then turn sharp right onto an unsigned narrow gated road, which is easily missed.

This delightfully quiet road of rough tarmac gives several steep climbs, punctuated by descents and gates. Ignore a minor turn right in favour of the lane continuing steeply uphill to the left, the final climb passing Cut-thorn House to bring you to a T-junction with the A53.

Turn left down the main road which gently undulates downhill for roughly 850m. At the far end of a plantation turn right towards Wildboarclough. This leads steeply downhill to a triangular junction by **Crag Hall** (a large country house. Bear right towards

163

Macclesfield Forest and head briefly uphill, before descending moderately steeply to **Clough House**.

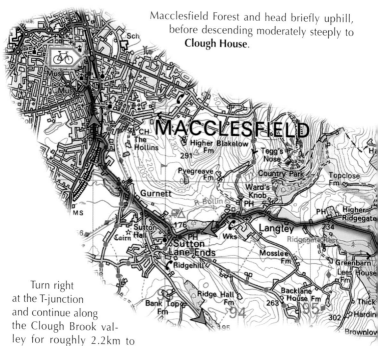

Turn right at the T-junction and continue along the Clough Brook valley for roughly 2.2km to **Bottom-of-the-oven**, ignoring a steep side-turn left in 1.5km. Sometimes there are llamas in the fields along this road. Take the second left towards Macclesfield Forest onto a quiet lane, heading moderately steeply up past Forest Lodge. Continue past a side turn right to Forest Chapel as the gradient eases.

Continue ahead to a T-junction, turning right and ignoring the bridleway straight ahead. Descend down a long hill, which is steep and narrow past **Trentabank Reservoir**, where herons may be seen. Continue downhill past Ridgegate Reservoir and bend left past Leathers Smithy PH. Pass a third reservoir and descend into **Langley** past St Dunstans Inn.

Bend right and downhill by the Methodist Church on Langley Road towards Sutton. In **Sutton**, bend right at the Church House PH to reach a T-junction and turn right towards Macclesfield on your outward route. Continue under the canal aqueduct past the Old Kings Head PH on Byrons Lane. Continue over the rail bridge and past the Railway View Inn.

Turn right onto the A523 and continue past the Travellers Rest PH. Bear left at the Sun Inn, then right at a major crossroads beside a park. Continue ahead over traffic lights and a pedestrian crossing to reach Macclesfield station.

↑ map
continued
from p163

ROUTE 21

TOUR DE PEAK DISTRICT

Grade	Multi-day challenge
Total distance	255km
Total ascent/descent	6235m
Parking	Parking for several nights is always going to be an issue in the Peak District. There is a large pay and display car park immediately outside the station, offering daily parking only. Alternative options include: using the train to arrive in Matlock, Marsden (Day 3) or Whaley Bridge (Day 4); starting the route in Derby using Bold Lane Secure Car Park (expensive, but ultra secure) and cycle or take the train to Matlock; starting the route from Whaley Bridge using the Canal Wharf Car Park (free, but own risk); starting at any point – the trail passes many rural and town-edge locations where you can park safely without inconvenience to residents, at your own judgement.
Cycle hire	See Appendix A for longer term hire options
Road bikes?	Most days are reasonable with detours, except Day 3 – see that day's route description
Accommodation	The inclusion of accommodation within the route description is not necessarily an endorsement, but a guide to what is available nearby.

A multiday challenge which sticks as close as is enjoyably possible to the boundary of the Peak District National Park.

This route is not intended to be a completely pure route – where the purist option would not give an enjoyable experience, and a more enjoyable alternative exists, the alternative will usually be taken. Purists (particularly technical mountain bikers) are welcome to devise their own version!

Experienced cyclists capable of riding more than 50km a day will likely wish to compress this route into three days – starting from Matlock, overnight stops at Marsden (102km) and Whaley Bridge (51km) with a final day of 102km, could be a useful starting point for redistributing the distance between days (bearing in mind that the original Day 3 is the toughest!).

DAY 1

Matlock to Dungworth	
Distance	51km
Ascent	1185m
Descent	1065m
Surface	93% road, 7% off-road
Start	Matlock railway station SK 296 602
Finish	Dungworth village SK 280 899

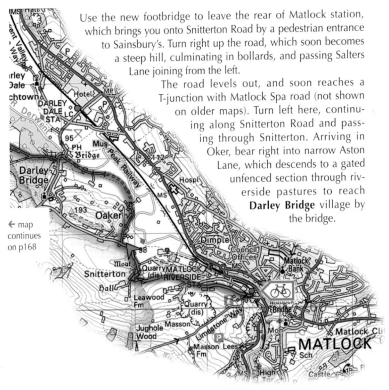

Use the new footbridge to leave the rear of Matlock station, which brings you onto Snitterton Road by a pedestrian entrance to Sainsbury's. Turn right up the road, which soon becomes a steep hill, culminating in bollards, and passing Salters Lane joining from the left.

The road levels out, and soon reaches a T-junction with Matlock Spa road (not shown on older maps). Turn left here, continuing along Snitterton Road and passing through Snitterton. Arriving in Oker, bear right into narrow Aston Lane, which descends to a gated unfenced section through riverside pastures to reach **Darley Bridge** village by the bridge.

← map
continues
on p168

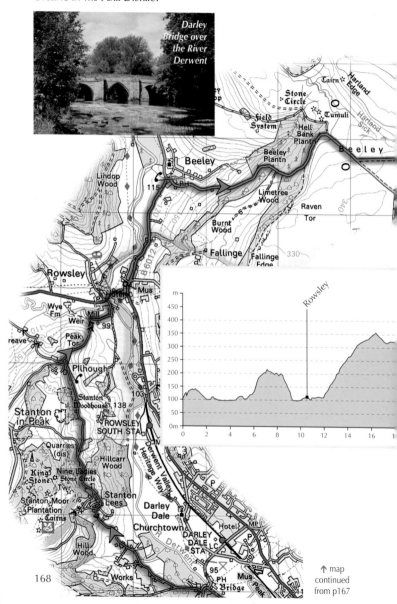

Darley Bridge over the River Derwent

↑ map continued from p167

map continues on p171

Route 21 Tour de Peak District Day 1

Turn left along the main road through the village, and after about 100m turn right onto Oldfield Lane, following a sign for Stanton in Peak. This road initially climbs moderately, levels out passing a large works on the left, then climbs again, culminating in a steep climb to a three-way junction at Stanton Lees. Turn right here for Stanton in Peak, and the gradient soon eases. Ignore a sharp left turn for Birchover and climb gently through Stanton Moor Quarries.

Take a minor right fork towards Pilhough, to descend gently along the hillside with wide views over the Derwent valley. At the crossroads hamlet of **Pilhough**, turn right down the steep hill towards Rowsley, taking care at the bends, and passing Cauldwell's Mill (café) to emerge onto the A6 in **Rowsley**.

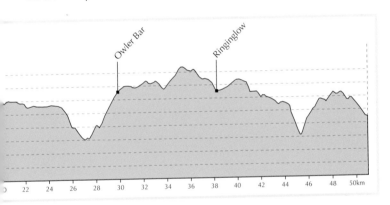

Turn right along the main road, and after roughly 250m turn left onto the B6012 towards Beeley. Follow this road for 2km then carefully turn right into **Beeley** at the foot of a left-bending dip. Pass the Devonshire Arms PH on your left, then begin a long climb through fields then plantations.

After about 3km, the road bends abruptly right away from the woods onto moorland, and 500m later brings you to a forked junction. Head left, then left again at a crossroads on **Beeley Moor**. Follow the undulating and bending road

↑ map
continues
on p172

for roughly 2km, then take a left turn towards Eastmoor. Ignore right turns a further 1km and 2km on, to reach the A619 above **Eastmoor**.

Cross straight over at this dangerous junction towards Cutthorpe. After about 600m cross over a major road, and in a further 1.3km turn right onto the B6050 towards Cutthorpe at a T-junction. At the bottom of a gentle descent bear left following a sign for Millthorpe. Follow this for 1.7km, ignoring a right turn after 1.2km, to reach a T-junction at SK 305 747. Turn left here for Millthorpe again, then turn right down a narrow lane, which gives a delightful wooded descent for 2.5km to **Cordwell**. Beware of horses on this lane.

At the bottom, turn left onto the B6051. Ignore a left fork early on, then rise up a 2.5km long climb to the **Owler Bar** gyratory roundabout. Take the second exit (B6054) towards Hathersage, rising gently for 2.8km to the A625. Turn right along this level road, before bearing left to give a gentle 750m of descent to the **Fox House** Inn.

Turn right towards Sheffield, and 500m later, as the gradient eases, fork left onto an unmade track, which soon passes through a gate at the entrance to Parson House.

Cyclist coming towards reader on the road below Stanton Moor

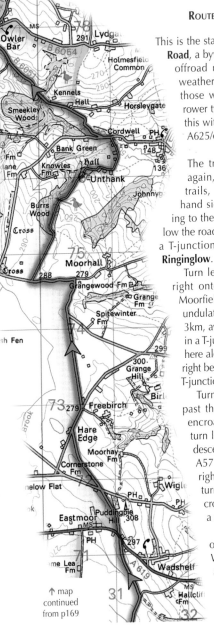

This is the start of the fantastic **Houndkirk Road**, a byway which gives 3km of great offroad riding (well drained in wet weather), requiring some care from those with less confidence or narrower tyres. **Road bikes** should avoid this with a 4.5km detour via A6187/ A625/country lane to Ringinglow.

The trail gently rises, falls and rises again, passes a moorland crossing of trails, before heading along the right hand side of a plantation and descending to the road. At the end of the trail, follow the road straight ahead for 150m to reach a T-junction opposite the Norfolk Arms at **Ringinglow**.

Turn left here, and almost immediately right onto Fulwood Lane, soon passing Moorfield Alpaca farm (café). Follow this undulating and winding lane for roughly 3km, avoiding all right turns, to culminate in a T-junction at the foot of a hill. Turn left here along Brown Hills Lane, taking a 90° right bend after 600m, to arrive at a further T-junction in 300m.

Turn right along Redmires Road and past the Three Merry Lads PH through encroaching housing. After about 2km turn left along Lodge Lane, which soon descends steeply with sharp bends to the A57 close to **Rivelin Mill Bridge**. Turn right here with care, and after 100m turn left along Rails Road. Soon you cross over another major road and up a steepening hill.

Bend right, then take the second of two sharp left turns onto Woodbank Road. This rises gently across the hillside for 800m, before

↑ map
continued
from p169

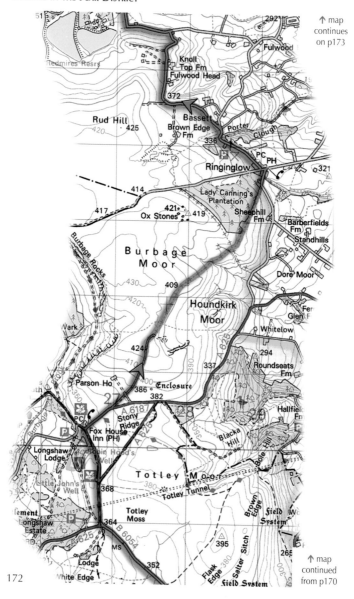

↑ map
continues
on p173

Redmires Resrs

Fulwood

Knoll
Top Fm
Fulwood Head

372

Rud Hill
420 • 425

Bassett
Brown Edge
Fm

Porter

Clough

338

PC PH

Ringinglow

321

414

Lady Canning's
Plantation

417

421 •
Ox Stones • 419

Sheephill
Fm

Barberfields
Fm

Standhills

Burbage
Moor

Burbage Rocks

430

420

409

Houndkirk
Moor

Dore Moor

Fern
Glen

Whitelow

Vark

424

294

Roundseats
Fm

Parson Ho

386

Enclosure

382

Hallfield
Fm

PC

A 618?

Stony
Ridge

Fox House
Inn (PH)

Blacka
Hill

Bole Hill

Longshaw
Lodge

Robin Hood's
Well

Little John's
Well

Totley Mo•o•r

368

Totley Tunnel

Brown
Edge

Field
System

Cement

Longshaw
Estate

364 B 6054

Totley
Moss

395

265

MS

Lodge

352

White Edge

Flask
Edge

Salter Sitch

Field System

↑ map
continued
from p170

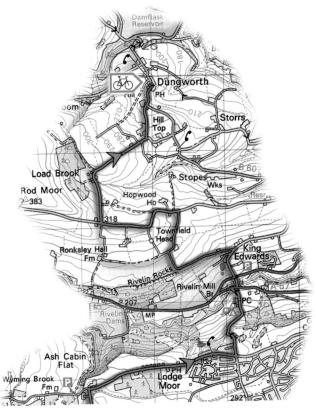

↑ map continued from p172

bending sharply right straight up the hillside for a final stretch before levelling out at a bend right. Turn left at a T-junction to pass Hopwood House, and after 1.3 km of gentle climbing, turn right towards Dungworth.

This first descends steeply to a sharp bend right and short climb, followed by a further descent to a left turn into Sykehouse Lane, which soon brings you down to a T-junction with the B6076 on the outskirts of **Dungworth**. Turn left here to reach the Royal Hotel in the village centre.

Riding up an easier section of the fabulous Houndkirk Road

WHERE TO STAY

As with many small Peak District villages, accommodation is limited, but there are a number of B&Bs as well as the Royal Hotel (PH with rooms), within a five mile radius.

B&Bs	Royal Hotel PH, Main Road, Dungworth S6 6HF ☎ 0114 285 1213 £
	Padley Farm B&B, Dungworth Green S6 6HE ☎ 0114 2851427 www.padleyfarm.co.uk £/££
	Loadbrook Farm B&B, Beeton Green, Nr Stannington S6 6GT ☎ 0114 234 3679 £
	Loadbrook Cottages B&B, Game Lane, Nr Stannington S6 6GT ☎ 0114 233 1619 £/££
	Rickett Field Farm B&B, Dungworth, Bradfield S6 6HA ☎ 0114 285 1218 £
Camping	Fox Hagg Farm, Lodge Lane, Rivelin S6 5SN ☎ 0114 230 5589 (6km south of Dungworth) April–October
	Thurlmoor Caravan Site, Carlecotes, Dunford Bridge S36 4TD ☎ 01226 762681 (8km W of Penistone, 34km beyond end Stage 1) March–October

DAY 2

Dungworth to Marsden	
Distance	51km
Ascent	1290m
Descent	1335m
Surface	85% road, 7% trail, 8% off-road
Start	Dungworth SK 280 899
Finish	Marsden SE 049 117

↑ map
continues
on p177

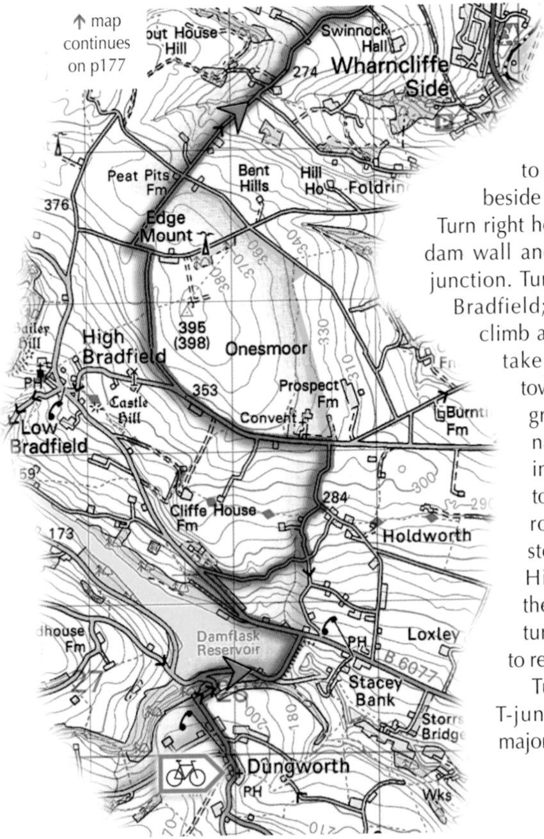

Leaving the Royal Hotel on your right, descend a steep hill with hairpins to reach a T-junction beside **Damflask Reservoir**. Turn right here to pass along the dam wall and reach a triangular junction. Turn left towards High Bradfield; the road starts to climb and after about 900m take a sharp right turn towards Holdworth. The gradient eases on this narrow lane, undulating across the hillside to reach a minor crossroads. Turn left here, steeply uphill towards High Bradfield. After the gradient has eased, turn left at a T-junction to resume the steep climb. Turn left at a further T-junction onto a more major road, past a convent,

175

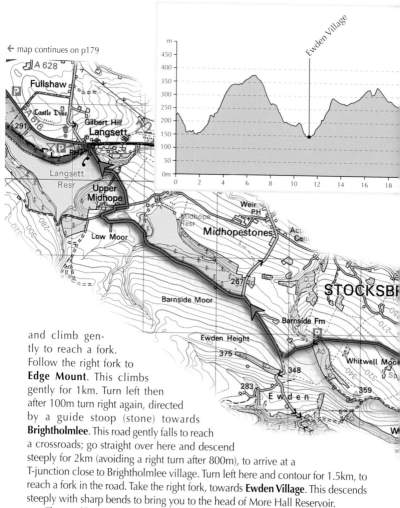

← map continues on p179

and climb gently to reach a fork.
Follow the right fork to
Edge Mount. This climbs
gently for 1km. Turn left then
after 100m turn right again, directed
by a guide stoop (stone) towards
Brightholmlee. This road gently falls to reach
a crossroads; go straight over here and descend
steeply for 2km (avoiding a right turn after 800m), to arrive at a
T-junction close to Brightholmlee village. Turn left here and contour for 1.5km, to
reach a fork in the road. Take the right fork, towards **Ewden Village**. This
descends steeply with sharp bends to bring you to the head of More Hall Reservoir.

The road bends right over a river bridge and soon comes to a highly skewed
crossroads with unsurfaced lanes. Take the sharp left turn, and through some
A-bars to gain a permissive path, which cycles may use by kind permission of the

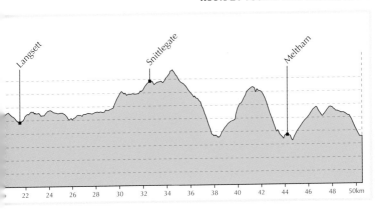

landowner, Yorkshire Water. (As with all permissive paths, this permission can be withdrawn at any time, in which case you will need to follow the road.) Follow the path uphill past the dam wall of Broomhead Reservoir to join another road. Turn right to climb the steepening hill to **Bolsterstone** village.

At the end of the main street, bear left onto a lane towards Midhopestones. Initially passing playing fields, ignore two right turns over the next 1.2km to reach a fork. Bear left here towards Strines, climbing and then steeply descending over Whitwell Moor to rise to a T-junction. Turn right here, enjoy a fast descent for 900m, but be ready to fork left at the end of the long straight towards Langsett. The road now descends more gently alongside a plantation, then gently ascends again with a sharp right turn to the hamlet of **Upper Midhope** after 2.7km.

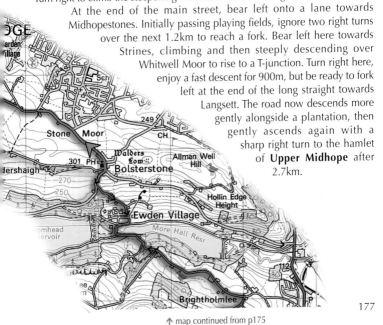

↑ map continued from p175

177

↑ map continued on p181

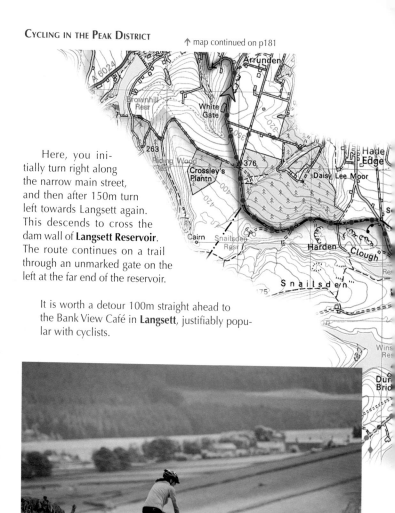

Here, you initially turn right along the narrow main street, and then after 150m turn left towards Langsett again. This descends to cross the dam wall of **Langsett Reservoir**. The route continues on a trail through an unmarked gate on the left at the far end of the reservoir.

It is worth a detour 100m straight ahead to the Bank View Café in **Langsett**, justifiably popular with cyclists.

Looking back over the valley before Upper Midhope

The gate at the end of the dam wall takes you along a new easy-going bridle-way, which may not be shown on some maps. After 200m beside the reservoir, follow zig-zags up the bank on the right where a footpath (only) continues straight ahead. At the top, turn left through a wall opening next to the car park, to follow a bridleway which continues gently climbing between reservoir plantations and road.

After 800m, having entered the plantation, bear left, then straight ahead, and then bear left at three junctions of trails on level ground, to bring you to a junction hanging on the edge of a shallow ravine. Turn right, following the bridleway sign for Flouch, and after 300m fork right onto a narrower trail which twists through woods to bring you to a crossing of the A628.

Go straight across the main road and follow a short muddy section through woods to reach the old Manchester road in 150m.

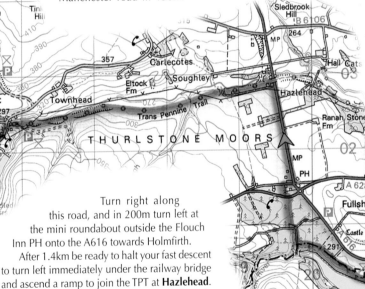

Turn right along this road, and in 200m turn left at the mini roundabout outside the Flouch Inn PH onto the A616 towards Holmfirth.

After 1.4km be ready to halt your fast descent to turn left immediately under the railway bridge and ascend a ramp to join the TPT at **Hazlehead**. At the top of the ramp go straight ahead along the trail; from here you have 4km of easy trail riding up the imperceptible gradient of the old railway line to **Dunford Bridge**.

↑ map
continued
from p176

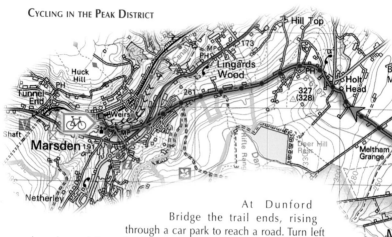

At Dunford Bridge the trail ends, rising through a car park to reach a road. Turn left along the road, immediately crossing a bridge over the final approach to the tunnel, and starting to climb steeply. After 700m, and at the end of the plantation on your right, turn right onto the Winscar Reservoir access road. Follow this road to the dam wall, bearing right to pass along this. Then head left along the east shore of the reservoir and through Broad Hill car park to to the top of the reservoir access road.

Turn left, then climb for a further 1.1km to reach **Snittlegate** crossroads just beyond the top. Turn left and follow this road for 3.8km, first gently climbing, then descending past a large plantation and onto a hillside traverse. Shortly after passing Coddy's Farm, bear left steeply downhill with hairpins on a road 'unsuitable for HGVs'. After the gradient has eased, look out for a school on the right; make a very sharp left turn opposite this along Dobbs Top Road; this soon bends down to a T-junction in **Holmbridge**. Turn right towards the church tower, and then in 100m turn right again along the A6024 past the church.

Cyclist near Snittlegate

Alternatively **keen mountain bikers** may choose to take a rough track left from where the plantation ends (SE 130 050), contouring past Crossley's Plantation, then descending steeply over rough terrain to Riding Wood Reservoir. Either take the road right past Brownhill Reservoir to rejoin the main route, or go past Yateholme Reservoir to reach the A6024, branching left in Holme village to rejoin the route at Digley Reservoir (SE 112 070).

After only 150m turn sharply left in front of the Bridge Tavern up Field End Lane. Climb steeply, bearing left after 500m onto Bank Top Lane, to reach **Digley Reservoir** after the same distance again. After the briefest of respites, the gradient becomes even steeper for a further 500m, past a car park to reach a crossroads. **Road cyclists** should continue ahead to avoid the Harden Moss bridleway. Take the left road, which briefly descends before resuming a healthy ascent for a further 1km to reach the A635.

Pass straight over the main road onto the stony driveway to Harden Moss Country House; at its gateway after 150m bear right down the wooded dip along a narrower track. Beyond the

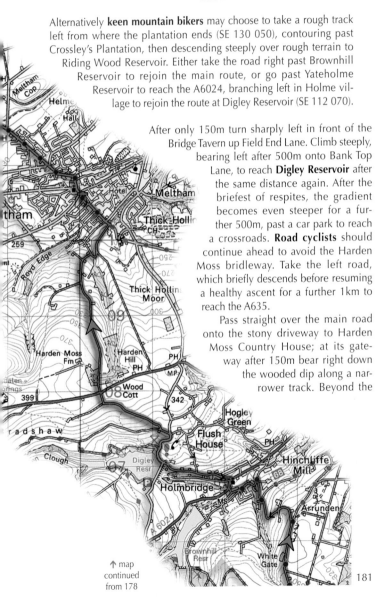

↑ map
continued
from 178

181

dip, the lane levels out, then begins a progressively steepening descent towards Meltham. An unexpected hazard on the steepest section of this interesting descent is a wooden hatch hiding the unknown! The unmade surface eventually gives way to tarmac, bending right and then leftwards at the bottom, to descend more gently to a T-junction with the B6107 at the bottom of a dip.

Turn left along the main road, rising steeply up the far side of the dip, then descending past the church in **Meltham** town centre to a mini roundabout by Morrison's supermarket in the bottom of a second dip. Here you bear left up Slaithwaite Road, which is still the B6107. The steep gradient soon eases a little, giving way to an unrelenting climb, passing the Traveller's Rest PH at the edge of town. You eventually reach a summit about 2km from the town centre, after which there is a short descent through a narrow, twisting dip at Holt Head, (where you avoid the right turn onto the B6109). The climb now resumes, soon levelling out as it bends around the moor edge, to then give a long descent into Marsden. At the bottom continue straight ahead at a highly skewed crossroads to soon reach the A62. Here cross straight over onto Brougham Road to reach **Marsden** town centre.

To reach the **rail station**, turn right by the Co-op, then follow this road across the river and bend left up the hill beyond.

WHERE TO STAY	
B&Bs	Surprisingly limited in the town, but try:
	Tunnel End Inn, Waters Road, Marsden HD7 6NF ☎ 01484 844636 www.tunnelendinn.com ££/£
	The Olive Branch (restaurant with rooms), Olive Terrace, Manchester Road, Marsden HD7 6LU ☎ 01484 844487 www.olivebranch.uk.com ££/£
	The Mistal, Cop Hill Side, Slaithwaite HD7 5XA ☎ 01484 845404 ££/£
Camping	Standedge Caravan and Campsite, The Carriage House, Manchester Road, Marsden HD7 6NL ☎ 01484 844419 www.carriage-house.co.uk
	Alternatively try searching on www.thefriendlyclub.co.uk

DAY 3

Marsden to Whaley Bridge	
Distance	51km
Total ascent	1480m
Total descent	1490m
Surface	64% road, 10% trail, 26% off-road
Start	Marsden SE 049 117
Finish	Whaley Bridge Rail Station SK 012 815

Road riders will struggle with this day's route – where pleasant country lanes form the boundary of the Peak District to the east, the geography is rather different on the west. The result is a choice of tougher off-road for those that prefer a purer route, or more A-roads/venturing further off the line of the national park boundary for those who prefer an easier route.

Space prohibits detail of a good road-biking alternative to the day, but linking Mossley–Stalybridge–Mottram–Charlesworth at the end of an easy-going trail section from Uppermill–Mossley, is probably the best alternative to the largest off-road section of the day (second PBW section).

To reach the start from Marsden station, head downhill and bend right to cross the Rover Colne into the town centre.

Facing the Co-op in **Marsden** Town Centre (opposite the end of Brougham Road), turn left up Peel Street. This soon takes you across the A62 to reach a T-junction with Carrs Road. Turn right here and in a further 300m you reach a crossroads, at which you go straight ahead up Mount Road. This lives up to its name, giving a long steep climb for 2.2km, with views of fine stone mills on your left, and passing the **golf club** at the edge of town.

↓ map
continues
on p185

183

The next section contains an off-road section (which is in the process of becoming part of a new bridleway link into the Pennine Bridleway) which crosses a council boundary. Oldham Council is happy it is now a bridleway but Kirklees Council (which covers the part from Mount Road to the stile near Standedge) insist it is still legally a footpath. However, the landowner (National Trust) believes it is already a bridleway and has no issues with responsible cyclists riding across it, so you shouldn't encounter any issues. But as always, if challenged, be polite, state the situation calmly and non-confrontationally, but be prepared to dismount or even deviate if need be.

The deviation continues up Mount Road road then runs left along a particularly dangerous part of the A62 over to Standedge Car Park.

Soon after Old Mount Road merges from the right, bear left onto a rough track which first crosses a gully, before making a sharp right turn to resume a course parallel with the road. You have now joined a new link to the Pennine Bridleway, (PBW). Follow the track uphill, gradually veering away from the road, with views of Redbrook Reservoir on the right, to reach a gate beside the A62 Standedge summit cutting. Bear left through the gate, to descend to the small **Standedge** car park after 300m.

From the car park, the new bridleway continues between the road and a small reservoir, passes through a gate and then descends the hillside beyond to join a more established rough track. You have now joined the PBW proper. Follow this track to the left and continue downhill for about 800m to reach a gate just above a farmhouse. Bear left through the gate, following a smoother track downhill at an easier grade for a similar distance, to emerge at a road junction next to the **Diggle** Hotel.

Take the road ahead past Kiln Green, which gives a steep uphill, then sweeps downhill to bear left at a triangular junction and up another steep hill. Approaching the top of this hill, follow the PBW with a right turn down a farm track. Bear left before the

↓ map
continues
on p186

↓ map
continued
from p183

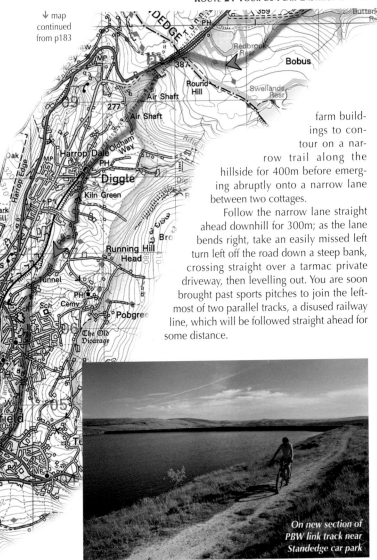

farm buildings to contour on a narrow trail along the hillside for 400m before emerging abruptly onto a narrow lane between two cottages.

Follow the narrow lane straight ahead downhill for 300m; as the lane bends right, take an easily missed left turn left off the road down a steep bank, crossing straight over a tarmac private driveway, then levelling out. You are soon brought past sports pitches to join the left-most of two parallel tracks, a disused railway line, which will be followed straight ahead for some distance.

*On new section of
PBW link track near
Standedge car park*

↓ map
continued
from p184

You will soon pass through a car park at Saddleworth Leisure Centre; from here you can detour for cafés on **Uppermill** main street, which is only 200m to the right of the trail.

There is a brief interruption to the trail at an awkward crossing of Higher Arthurs, followed soon afterwards by the A669 and another minor road. Here you briefly follow Croft Edge; at its end follow the trail straight ahead, crossing a footbridge and climbing briefly. At a junction of trails above, turn right and leave the PBW for a while. However, the keen off-roader can continue along the PBW, to rejoin the described route at Carrbrook.

Continue on the trail along a pleasant wooded riverside for a further 1km. Here you emerge close to the crossroads of the A635 and B6175. You will cross both these roads to regain the trail, signed as a bridleway for Mossley via Roaches.

After a further 1.8km, the rail trail ends, joining a road at a restored station building. Continue straight ahead down Station Road, cross straight over Micklehust Road in 100m, then almost immediately left up Staley Road.

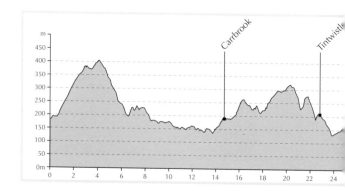

Follow this uphill to reach the B6175. Turn right along the main road through Heyheads, and then turn left at traffic lights up School Lane. This very narrow lane bends, passes through a gate and ends with a right fork past a school to emerge in **Carrbrook** village at a mini roundabout.

Go straight over this and up South View, soon arriving at another roundabout. Turn right here, entering Stalybridge Country Park and regaining the PBW, which you will now be following as far as Tintwistle. The tarmac gives way first to cobbles, and then bends right up a lane surfaced with unusual long-end-on slabs. The surface becomes rougher for a while but soon eases and levels out to contour along the hillside with wide views. Avoid the temptation to take a better surfaced right fork downhill after 1km. The trail soon descends roughly to a junction of tarmac tracks above **Walkerwood Reservoir**.

Pass through a gate and bear left to begin a long gentle tarmac climb past further reservoirs for 1.6km to pass along the dam wall of **Upper Swineshaw**

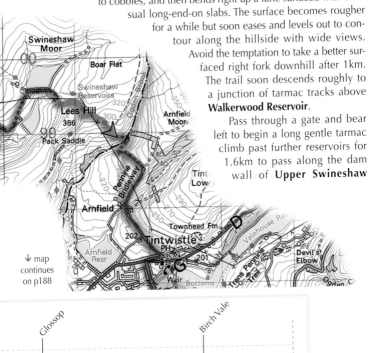

↓ map
continues
on p188

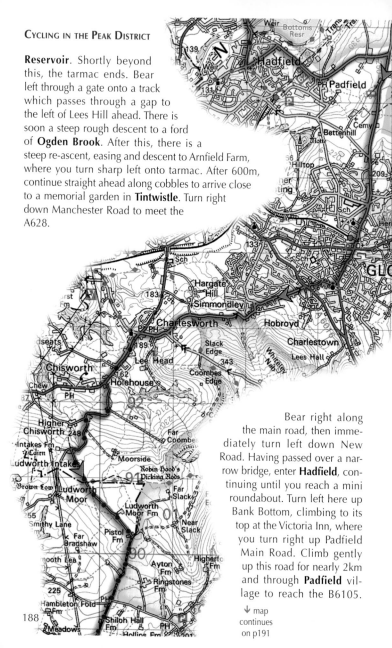

Reservoir. Shortly beyond this, the tarmac ends. Bear left through a gate onto a track which passes through a gap to the left of Lees Hill ahead. There is soon a steep rough descent to a ford of **Ogden Brook**. After this, there is a steep re-ascent, easing and descent to Arnfield Farm, where you turn sharp left onto tarmac. After 600m, continue straight ahead along cobbles to arrive close to a memorial garden in **Tintwistle**. Turn right down Manchester Road to meet the A628.

Bear right along the main road, then immediately turn left down New Road. Having passed over a narrow bridge, enter **Hadfield**, continuing until you reach a mini roundabout. Turn left here up Bank Bottom, climbing to its top at the Victoria Inn, where you turn right up Padfield Main Road. Climb gently up this road for nearly 2km and through **Padfield** village to reach the B6105.

↓ map
continues
on p191

188

↓ map
continued
from p187

Looking down on Arnfield Brook on PBW below Lees Hill

Turn right here, descending for 2.5km into **Glossop**, passing the railway station to arrive at a major crossroads.

Cross straight over, following the A624 uphill towards Hayfield. As the gradient eases and the main road bends left, bear right up James Street directly towards the church. At the T-junction in front of the church, turn right and then take the first left down Slatelands Road, following this down over a bridge with bollards and up to the A6106. Turn right and then immediately left to gain Simmondley New Road and climb steeply to Simmondley village green, some 750m distant. Turn left and uphill again, passing the Hare & Hounds PH, to climb and then descend over 1.8km to meet the A626 in **Charlesworth** outside the Grey Mare PH.

Turn left along the main road, descending to the start of Chisworth and turn left up New Mills Road at the bottom, as the main road bends right. This narrow lane winds steeply uphill. Ignore a right turn, and then take a left turn towards Rowarth to bring you to plateau level in 1.4km. Continue ahead for about 3km along the ridge, passing **Pistol Farm** at a narrow bend. Ignore a dead end left turn to arrive at a T-junction with Moor End Road. Turn left here, and almost immediately bear left and downhill on Briargrove Road.

Descend steeply to cross the river bridge at the bottom, gently climbing to a point where the road bends right in woodland. Here bear left up the lane which goes past **Aspenshaw Hall**, continuing as a bridleway after the last farm building. This steep and narrow section will challenge the skilled to keep their feet off the ground! At its top, the bridleway joins a track; turn right along this to

189

descend gradually to rejoin the road at a T-junction. Turn right to descend to Thornsett then turn sharp left down Sycamore Road into **Birch Vale**, climbing beyond the dip to reach the A6015 outside the Grouse PH.

Turn right along the main road, and 250m later bear left and steeply uphill opposite a converted chapel. The lane climbs steeply past quarries, eventually giving way to a rough track contouring the hillside. The track joins a tarmac road on a sharp bend roughly 3km from Birch Vale. Bear right steeply down the road to reach a T-junction by Brookdale Cattery; turn left here to descend more gently into **Buxworth**.

> The observant map reader will notice that there is a 20km long and narrow tongue of **industrial land** projecting into the Peak District, which extends from New Mills to the quarries south of Buxton. Our route cuts across this, but the purist is welcome to devise their own variation which follows the border more accurately!

Turn right along the B6062, under the railway bridge and past the primary school and then turn left into Brookside following R68. Cross the canal and A6 bridges and immediately turn right up Silk Hill. Climb and later descend steeply to reach a T-junction with Old Road in **Whaley Bridge**. Turn right, soon joining the A5004 outside the Shepherds Arm. Turn right again to find the railway station in 200m.

WHERE TO STAY	
B&Bs	Kinrara, Macclesfield Road, Whaley Bridge SK23 7DR ☎ 01663 734587 www.kinrara-bedandbreakfast.co.uk £
	Springbank, 3 Reservoir Road, Whaley Bridge SK23 7BL ☎ 01663 732819 www.whaleyspringbank.co.uk £/££
	Spire House, Bings Road, Whaley Bridge SK23 7ND ☎ 01663 73319 www.spirehouse.co.uk £
Camping	Ringstones Caravan Park, Yeardsley Lane, Furness Vale SK23 7EB ☎ 01663 732152 or 07790 428953 March–October
	or search www.thefriendlyclub.co.uk

↓ map
continued
from p188

191

↓ map
continues
on p194

Restored station platform at Nelson's Pit (Middlewood Way)

DAY 4

Whaley Bridge to Blackshaw Moor	
Distance	50km
Ascent	1220m
Descent	1140m
Surface	88% road, 9% trail, 3% off-road
Start	Whaley Bridge SK 012 815
Finish	Blackshaw Moor SK 009 598 (or detour into Leek for wider choice of accommodation)

Facing the railway station, take Reservoir Road under the bridge immediately to the left of the station. After the bridge, follow the main road right, which becomes Whaley Lane. The steep ascent brings you to the 315m summit, followed by a long descent to the A6 at **Disley**, some 5.5km from the start.

Cross straight over the main road at traffic lights into Jacksons Edge Road. After 1.3km of climb and gentle descent, turn right into Wybersley Road just before the descent steepens. Follow this ridge-top road with fine views for 2.5km, passing Dove House Farm early on. Returning into housing, turn left for Hawk Green, and at the crossroads by the Crown PH 300m later, turn left along Windlehurst Road.

Pass over a narrow canal bridge and 400m later, at **Doodfield** Stores, turn right along Torkington Lane towards

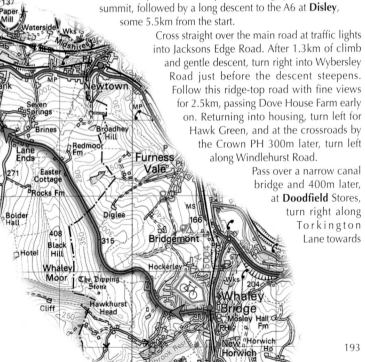

↓ map
continued
from p192

Hazel Grove. A number of bends bring you to a bridge over the Middlewood Way (R55) rail trail. You need to carry on for a further 300m here, to where the road bends abruptly right, and you take a narrow entry left between two houses to join the Middlewood Way.

Turn right along the trail for about 4km. The restored station platforms at **Higher Poynton** (Nelson's Pit) are a good spot for a picnic, or short detour to the 'Coffee Tavern' or pub. Only 600m beyond this, the trail narrows to accommodate a car park on the left; leave the trail here and bear right along the parallel road.

This lane soon passes under the canal in an unusual tunnel, then climbs steeply and undulates past another 'Coffee Tavern' to reach a T-junction on a steep hill after 3km. Turn left

↓ map
continues
on p195

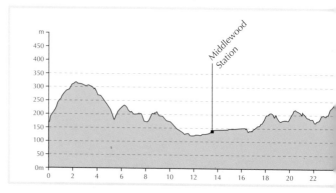

and uphill towards **Pott Shrigley**; the road soon levels and descends to bend right past Pott Shrigley Church. After a further 300m take a left fork, Spulley Lane, towards Rainow.

This is a good point to detour into **Bollington** if you wish. (NB Cafés are surprisingly hard to find in Bollington, but Café Waterside (closed Mon) is a good one – by the canal visitor centre in an old mill building, SJ 934 872).

The road descends to a dip and then climbs again to reach a triangular junction. Bear left and steeply uphill to enter Oakenbank Lane.

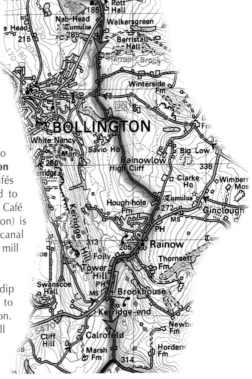

↓ map continues on p196

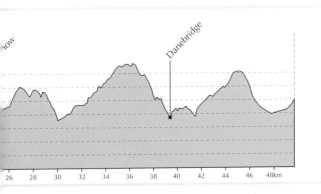

195

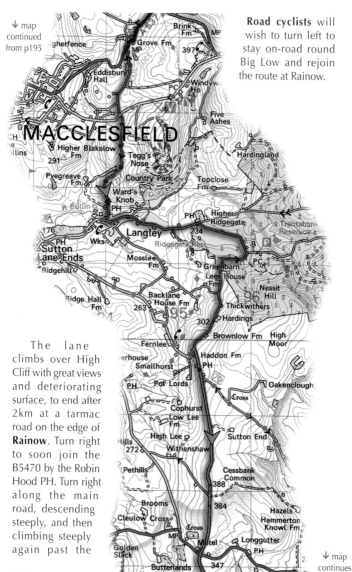

Road cyclists will wish to turn left to stay on-road round Big Low and rejoin the route at Rainow.

The lane climbs over High Cliff with great views and deteriorating surface, to end after 2km at a tarmac road on the edge of **Rainow**. Turn right to soon join the B5470 by the Robin Hood PH. Turn right along the main road, descending steeply, and then climbing steeply again past the

↓ map continued from p195

↓ map continues on p198

Riding up the surprisingly steep Bull Hill Lane towards Walker Barn

unusual folly on Tower Hill. As the road levels out, it bends right and uphill again by a small triangular green (Mount Pleasant); ignore this and bear left (even steeper) up Penny Lane towards Buxton. Grind up the steep hill (which becomes Bull Hill Lane) for 1km to reach a T-junction with the A537.

Turn right down the main road. Immediately after some sharp bends bear left up the very narrow Back Eddisbury Road. This climbs steeply, and soon descends to a staggered crossroads in the bottom of a dip. Dog-leg left then right into Broadcar Road, which after a short climb gives a steep, narrow and twisting descent into **Langley**. Turn left at the T-junction, then fork left almost immediately after at the church towards Macclesfield Forest. The road climbs past one reservoir to reach the Leathers Smithy PH at the dam of Ridgegate Reservoir.

Follow the road right along the reservoir side, and at the reservoir end turn right down a narrow lane towards Wincle. Climb steeply at times, to emerge after 1.8km onto a more major road at a sharp bend. Turn left and uphill, passing the Hanging Gate PH, ignoring a left turn taken by the Cheshire Cycleway. The road climbs more gently with good views right for 2.5km, to descend to the Motel at the crossroads with the A54.

Go straight over the main road. Ignore side turns on the steep descent through **Wincle** to **Danebridge**, after which gravity takes its revenge with a long but gentle climb. Shortly after the west lodge of Swythamley Hall, take the major road left at a fork, to keep climbing and pass a private chapel after roughly 600m.

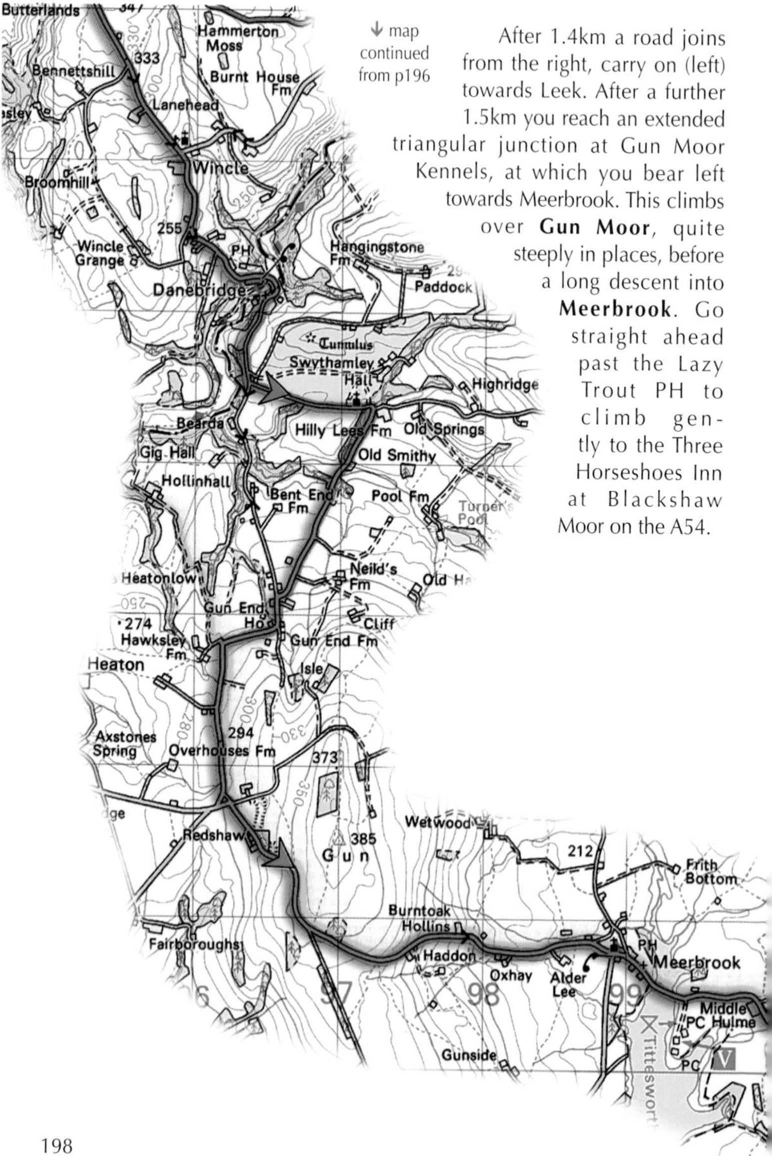

↓ map
continued
from p196

After 1.4km a road joins from the right, carry on (left) towards Leek. After a further 1.5km you reach an extended triangular junction at Gun Moor Kennels, at which you bear left towards Meerbrook. This climbs over **Gun Moor**, quite steeply in places, before a long descent into **Meerbrook**. Go straight ahead past the Lazy Trout PH to climb gently to the Three Horseshoes Inn at Blackshaw Moor on the A54.

WHERE TO STAY	
B&B	Three Horseshoes Inn, Blackshaw Moor, ST13 8TW ☎ 01538 300296 www.3shoesinn.co.uk. ££ This is pricey, so you may wish to detour into Leek for accommodation, following Route 11 from Meerbrook into Leek, and the next day rejoining the route at Thorncliffe or Morridge.
	At Waterhouses (17km further on) – both PHs up for sale/closed at time of writing but hoping to reopen:
	The George Inn, Leek Road, Waterhouses, ST10 3HW ☎ 01538 308804
	Ye Olde Crown PH, Leek Road, Waterhouses, ST10 3HL ☎ 01538 308204
Campsites	Leek Camping and Caravanning Club Site, Blackshaw Grange, Blackshaw Moor ST13 8TL ☎ 0845 1307633

Cyclist on the country lane towards Wincle from Ridgegate Reservoir

DAY 5

Blackshaw Moor to Matlock	
Distance	53km
Ascent	1060m
Descent	1205m
Surface	93% road, 7% off-road
Start	Blackshaw Moor SK 009 598
Finish	Matlock Railway Station SK 296 602

From the Three Horseshoes at **Blackshaw Moor**, turn right along the main road, and after 100m turn left towards Thorncliffe. The road climbs gently towards the village, where it descends briefly to an awkward T-junction in **Thorncliffe** village. Turn sharp left and steeply uphill here, embarking immediately on the steep 1.5km long climb up to the ridgeline. At the summit junction take Blakelow Road to the right, which sets you on course for the long traverse along **Morridge**, with wide panoramic views either side.

The long undulating ridge line of Morridge

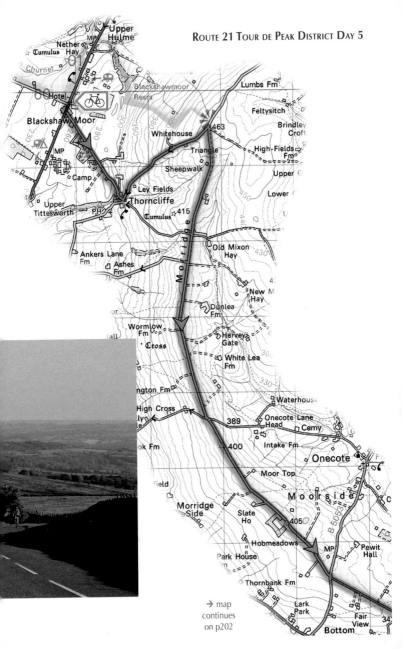

Upper
Hulme

Nether
Hay

Cumulus

Churnet

Blackshawmoor
Resr

Lumbs Fm

Feltysitch

Hotel

Whitehouse

463

Brindley
Croft

High-Fields
Fm

Blackshaw Moor

Triangle

Upper C

MP

Sheepwalk

Lower

Camp

Ley Fields

Upper
Tittesworth

Thorncliffe

PH

Cumulus ∴ 415

Ankers Lane
Fm

Old Mixon
Hay

Ashes
Fm

New
Hay

Dunlea
Fm

Wormlow
Fm

Harvey
Gate

Cross

White Lea
Fm

ngton Fm

Waterhouse

High Cross

389

Onecote Lane
Head

Cemy

ok Fm

400

Intake Fm

Onecote

field

Moor Top

Moorside

Morridge
Side

Slate
Ho

405

Hobmeadows

MP

Pewit
Hall

Park House

Thornbank Fm

Lark
Park

Fair
View

Bottom

→ map
continues
on p202

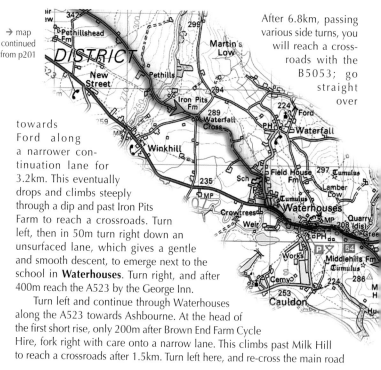

→ map
continued
from p201

After 6.8km, passing various side turns, you will reach a cross-roads with the B5053; go straight over

towards Ford along a narrower continuation lane for 3.2km. This eventually drops and climbs steeply through a dip and past Iron Pits Farm to reach a crossroads. Turn left, then in 50m turn right down an unsurfaced lane, which gives a gentle and smooth descent, to emerge next to the school in **Waterhouses**. Turn right, and after 400m reach the A523 by the George Inn.

Turn left and continue through Waterhouses along the A523 towards Ashbourne. At the head of the first short rise, only 200m after Brown End Farm Cycle Hire, fork right with care onto a narrow lane. This climbs past Milk Hill to reach a crossroads after 1.5km. Turn left here, and re-cross the main road

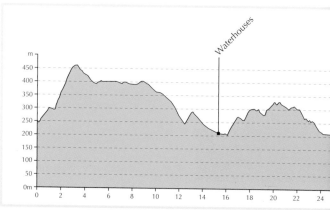

towards Calton at another crossroads after 200m. There's a gentle descent to a further crossroads at the edge of **Calton Green**. Here, turn right and uphill towards Calton Moor, which brings you back to the A523 in a further 1.6km.

Turn left along the main road and after 100m left again opposite the junction with the A52. This 6km road initially undulates and then gives a narrow descent. Ignore all side turns and continue past **Blore** and Okeover Hall to arrive in **Mapleton**. Turn right towards Ashbourne, passing the Okeover Arms PH in the village. After 2km you will pass a car park on the Tissington Trail, from where you can detour into **Ashbourne** (cafés) through the railway tunnel.

After the car park, continue up the hill to end at a T-junction on the outskirts of the town. Turn left here along North Avenue, soon reaching a crossroads with the A515. Go straight over the main road onto Windmill

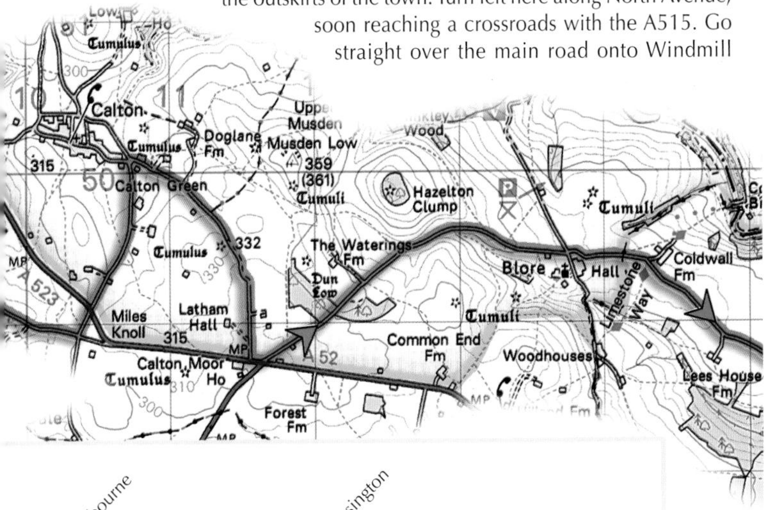

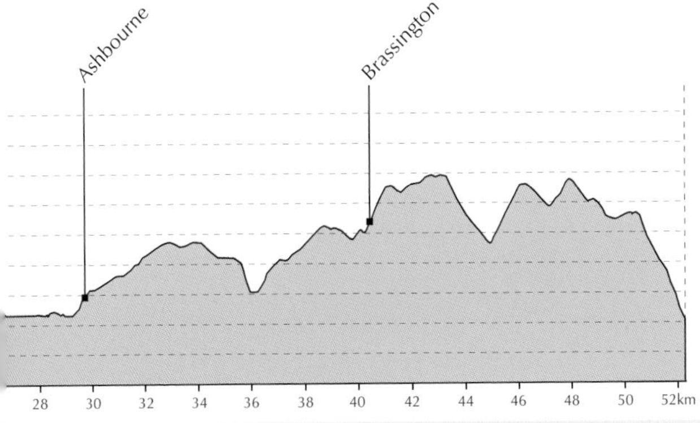

→ map
continues
on p204

203

Crossing Okeover Bridge near Mapleton, Ashbourne

Lane, which climbs gently and pleasantly to reach the B5035.
Go straight ahead (left) along the main road for a further
2km. Pass the Ketch PH and 600m later bear left on a
minor lane towards Knivetonwood.

→ map
continued
from p203

204

→ map
continues
on p206

Road cyclists should continue through **Kniveton** and left by The Knockerdown PH to Bradbourne.

After 700m turn left at Knivetonwood Farm down a lane which is easily confused as a farm turning only. This deteriorates over the next 900m as it passes two farms; after the second it becomes a grassy lane which continues straight through a gate into fields. Some parts of the final descent to the B5035 (close to the ford) are steep and rough.

Turn right along the main road, and 350m later turn right again up the hill to **Bradbourne**. At the far end of the village 1km later, bear left to **Brassington**, which you will reach after 3km of gentle climb and descent. Arriving outside the Miners Arms, bear left along the level line, and follow this for a short distance to a T-junction with the main road through the village. Turn left and steeply uphill to **Longcliffe**, passing under a bridge (PBW/HPT) beyond the summit.

At the crossroads soon after, pass straight over the B5056, to reach a right turn next to a lorry park 600m later. Turn right here towards **Aldwark**. After 1km turn sharp right to descend steeply for a further 1.4km before merging with the B5056 for the final 200m to the Holly Bush Inn at **Grangemill**.

Pass straight over the A5012 and almost immediately turn right towards Ible. Follow this road steeply uphill,

On the way into Bradbourne village

ignoring the right turn for Ible, and past Tophill Farm to arrive at a desolate moortop junction (SK 253 578). Turn left, soon losing the tarmac and passing an abandoned barn, to gently descend through mineworkings on a rough surface to meet a crossing of a tarmac road (SK 255 584).

Go straight over, descending then gradually climbing on a rougher surface to meet another track at a T-junction (SK 262 588). Turn left here to climb more steeply and eventually rejoin tarmac for the last time. Turn right, passing through **Brightgate** to descend a narrow lane for 1km and reach a junction.

Turn left. This soon becomes a final steep and narrow descent into **Matlock**. As you reach the first houses of the town, the road appears to take you left and uphill again; this is avoided by going right through bollards to complete the descent to Matlock Railway Station on Snitterton Road.

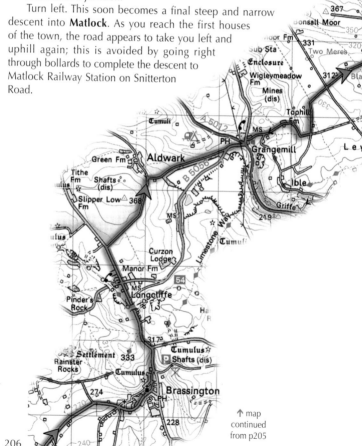

↑ map
continued
from p205

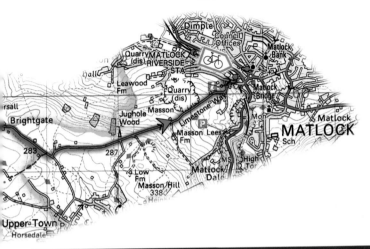

WHERE TO STAY	
B&B	B&Bs in Matlock tend to be pricey: the following are good quality, rather than 'cyclist on a budget friendly'.
	Ellen House, 37 Snitterton Road DE4 3LZ ☎ 01629 55584 www.ellenhousebandbmatlock.co.uk ££
	Riverbank Guest House, Derwent Avenue DE4 3LX ☎ 01629 582593 www.riverbankhouse.co.uk ££
	Cables B&B, 182 Dale Road DE4 3PS ☎ 01629 583629 www.the-cablesbandb.co.uk ££
	Sheriff Lodge, Dimple Road DE4 3JX ☎ 01629 760760 www.sherifflodge.co.uk ££
	Yew Tree Cottage, The Knoll, Tansley DE4 5FP ☎ 01629 583862, 07799 541903 www.yewtreecottagebb.co.uk (5km E of Matlock – but much cheaper and v recommended) £
Campsites	Barn Farm, Birchover DE4 2BL ☎ 01629 650245 www.barnfarmcamping.com (5km W of Matlock)
	Lickpenny Caravan Park, Lickpenny Lane, Tansley DE4 5GF ☎ 01629 583040 www.lickpennycaravanpark.co.uk (5km E of Matlock)

APPENDIX A
CYCLE HIRE

There are two types of cycle hire centre – those that deliver bikes to you within a certain region (usually best for multi-day hire of more than one bike), and those where you collect the bike (usually best for single day hire of one or two bikes). For all hire centres, proof of identity and a deposit (typically £10–£20) may be required, and helmets may or may not be provided – check with the individual centre for more information. A pump and (perhaps) a limited toolkit (enough to change a punctured inner tube) should also be provided but you may need to ask for these.

Delivered to you
Throughout the Peak District:

Peak Tours (Cycle Hire and Delivery in Peak District, Derbyshire and Manchester areas)

☎ 01457 651462   07961 052590
Email: info@peak-tours.com
Web: www.peak-tours.com

Prices: £13–£18 full day/
£45–£55 week (adults) £10 full day/
£30 week (childrens) bikes

Plus £5–£15 per delivery (depending on distance from Glossop)

Minimum Order £40,
free delivery over £70

Opening hours: 9am–6pm every day.

Greater Manchester/W Yorks region:

Wheelie Fun Mountain Bike Hire
Lee Mill Road, Hebden Bridge HX7 8LJ
☎ 07952 654617

Prices: from £20 a day, delivered and collected in Greater Manchester/ W Yorks area.

'Collect From' Hire Centres
Peak Cycle Hire

Operated by Peak District National Park/ Derbyshire County Council:
see individual centre listings below or www.peakdistrict.gov.uk/index/ visiting/cycle

Prices: £15 for full day (adult bikes), £10 for full day (child bikes)

Open: Everyday 9.30am–5.30pm Mar– Oct; limited winter opening

Derwent – Fairholmes (Routes 3 Ashopton, 5 Bamford, 17 Bamford)
Fairholmes Car Park, Derwent,
Bamford S33 0AQ
☎ 01433 651261
www.peakdistrict.gov.uk/index/visiting/ cycle/cycle-hire-centres/derwent.htm

Ashbourne (Routes 6 Ashbourne, 8 Tissington)
Tissington Trail, Mapleton Lane,
Ashbourne, Derbyshire DE6 2AA
☎ 01335 343156
www.peakdistrict.gov.uk/index/visiting/ cycle/cycle-hire-centres/ashbourne.htm

Parsley Hay (Routes 8 Tissington, 9 Wirksworth, 15 Buxton, 4 Middlewood, 18 Middlewood, 20 Macclesfield)
High Peak Trail, Parsley Hay SK17 0DG
☎ 01298 84493
www.peakdistrict.gov.uk/index/visiting/ cycle/cycle-hire-centres/parsleyhay.htm

Middleton Top (Route 9 Wirksworth)
Middleton Top Cycle Hire Centre,
Middleton-by-Wirksworth DE4 4LS
☎ 01629 823204

Other hire centres (south to north)

Carsington Sport and Leisure
(Route 2 Carsington Water)
☎ 01628 540478
www.carsingtonwater.com,
enquiries@carsingtonwater.com

Prices: £6/1hr, £8/2hrs, £15 all day

Open: 10am–5.30pm summer, closing earlier in winter

Hassop Station Cycle Hire (Routes 5
Bamford, 10 Bakewell, 14 Tideswell,
15 Buxton, 16 Grindleford, 17 Bamford)
Bakewell DE45 1NW
(1.6km N of Bakewell on the A6020/
B6001 roundabout)
☎ 01629 815668
duncan@hassopstation.co.uk

Open: 9am–5pm, 7 days a week: cycle hire should be available by Easter 2011.

Brown End Farm Cycle Hire
(Routes 11 Leek, 12 Waterhouses)
Waterhouses ST10 3JR
☎ 01538 308313
www.manifoldcycling-brownendfarm.
co.uk, sriley01@gmail.com

Open: Easter–End Sept 9.30am–6.30pm:
other times by arrangement

Prices: £11.50 adults/£7.50 children
(all day), no credit cards, free helmet use
and parking for hirers

Manifold Cycles (Routes 11 Leek,
12 Waterhouses)
The Manifold Track Cycle Hire Centre,
Old Station Car Park, Earlsway,
Waterhouses ST10 3EG
☎ 01538 308609

Open: School holidays and weekends
during Easter–Oct and all of July (ring to
see if they're open outside these times)

Prices: £15 adults/£7.50 children (all day)

Trail Monkeys (Routes 5 Bamford,
14 Tidesworth, 16 Grindleford,
17 Bamford)
Netherside, Bradwell S33 9JL
☎ 01433 621533
www.trailmonkeys.co.uk or
www.hikebikeandride.com

Open: 10am–6pm, every day.
(Opens earlier from 9am on Fr, Sa, Mo)

Prices: £25 adult (all day)

Longdendale Valley Cycles (Routes
4 Middlewood, 18 Middlewood,
19 Marsden, 20 Macclesfield)
Hikers and Bikers (below Café Royston)
105 Station Road, Hadfield SK13 1AA
☎ 01457 854672 or 07973 376124
www.hikers-and-bikers.co.uk/
longdendale-valley-cycles
annetteinhadfield@yahoo.co.uk

Open: 9am–7pm (or dark) every day

Prices: £15 adults/children (all day).
Helmets **not** provided

Pot House Hamlet (Route 13 Penistone)
Pot House Hamlet, Silkstone,
Barnsley S75 4JU
☎ 01226 790441
www.pothousehamlet.co.uk,
info@pothousehamlet.co.uk

Open: 10am–5pm every day

This organisation plans to offer cycle hire
– but please contact Tom at Pot House
Hamlet for more recent information on
opening status and prices.

ROUTES WITHOUT NEARBY CYCLE HIRE		
Route 1	Chesterfield	nearest is Hassop Station
Route 4	Middlewood	nearest is Peak Tours or Longdendale Valley Cycles
Route 7	Chesterfield	nearest is Hassop Station
Route 13	Penistone	nearest is Pot House Hamlet or Peak Tours
Route 15	Buxton	nearest is Hassop Station or TrailMonkeys
Route 16	Grindleford	nearest is Hassop Station or TrailMonkeys
Route 18	Middlewood	nearest is Peak Tours or Longdendale Valley
Route 19	Marsden	nearest is Peak Tours, Wheelie Fun or Longdendale Valley.
Route 20	Macclesfield	nearest is Peak Tours or Longdendale Valley
Route 21	Day 1 Matlock	nearest is Middleton Top or Hassop Station
Route 21	Day 2 Dungworth	nearest is Pot House Hamlet or Peak Tours
Route 21	Day 3 Marsden	nearest is Peak Tours, Wheelie Fun or Longdendale Valley
Route 21	Day 4 Whaley Bridge	nearest is Peak Tours or Longdendale Valley
Route 21	Day 5 Blackshaw Moor	nearest is Manifold Cycles or Brown End Farm Cycle Hire

APPENDIX B
CYCLES AND TRAINS

Where practical, the routes in this guide-book railway stations as starting points, so those who would prefer to leave the car at home (or are visiting without one, or without a bike-rack) have the best possible options for this.

Readers who are used to efficient and user-friendly facilities for taking cycles on trains in other countries should beware of Britain's notoriously inconsistent and often user-hostile offerings! You may encounter the following issues.

- There are several different train operating companies, who often have different and conflicting policies regarding cycles

- A single rail route may be used by two or more companies with different policies

- Cycles are commonly limited to two per train

- Tandems are very rarely carried at all

- Cycles often need to be reserved in advance onto specific trains

- Internet and telephone services for general ticket sales are unable to perform cycle reservations – you may need to visit a station in person, with the ticket you bought online, to make a cycle reservation

- Some services, by contrast, are non-reservable, the spaces being filled on a first-come, first-served basis

- A non-reservable first stage of your journey may jeopardise later connections requiring a reservation

- Oh, and by the way, don't even **think** about taking a bike onto a bus!

However, having initially painted a grim picture, you will in practice find that long journeys can successfully be completed with a little patience, and that the strict company policies are in practice implemented much more leniently by their staff on the ground.

National Rail provide a useful pdf leaflet, www.nationalrail.co.uk/passenger_services/2010CyclingbyTrain.pdf, about carrying cycles on trains.

The **AtoB** website www.atob.org.uk/Bike_Rail.html is also a useful source of current train operators cycle policies and gives some hints on which are more cycle-friendly than others.

East Coast Trains' website www.eastcoast.co.uk allows cycle reservations on all train operators' services. See below for more details.

Individual train operators (2010)

East Midlands Trains ☎ 08457 125678, www.eastmidlandstrains.co.uk, cycle.reservations@eastmidlandstrains.co.uk

Covers the SE and E of the region:

- Derby to Sheffield
- Derby/Nottingham to Matlock
- Manchester to Sheffield/Nottingham

Reservations are not possible on the Matlock line, but should be made on both the Derby to Sheffield and Manchester-Sheffield-Nottingham routes (including Hope Valley stations).

Cross Country ☎ 0844 8110124, www.crosscountrytrains.co.uk/Customer_service/Cyclists.aspx, customer.relations@crosscountrytrains.co.uk

CYCLING IN THE PEAK DISTRICT

Covers E and SW of the region

- Derby to Sheffield (via Chesterfield)
- Stoke on Trent to Manchester (via Macclesfield)

Reservations strongly recommended.

Transpennine ☎ 0845 6001674
www.tpexpress.co.uk

Covers NW and N of the region

- Manchester Airport to Sheffield,
- Manchester to Stalybridge

Reservations recommended, but don't appear to be possible.

Northern ☎ 0845 0000125 (enquiries), 0845 6008008 (reservations), www.northernrail.org, customer.relations@northernrail.org

Covers NW to NE of the region

- Manchester (Victoria) to Stalybridge, Marsden and Huddersfield
- Manchester (Piccadilly) to Hadfield, Glossop and Broadbottom
- Manchester (Piccadilly) to New Mills, Edale, Grindleford, Sheffield
- Manchester (Piccadilly) to Disley, New Mills, Whaley Bridge, Buxton
- Sheffield to Penistone, Denby Dale and Huddersfield
- Stoke on Trent to Manchester via Macclesfield.

Reservations not required, and train staff tend to be friendly and as helpful as possible, although peak trains may get full quickly.

Virgin ☎ 08719 774222 (bike bookings), 08457 222 333 (ticket line), www.virgintrains.com, customer.relations@virgintrains.co.uk

Covers W of the region

- Stoke on Trent to Manchester via Macclesfield

Services carry up to four bikes (yay!); very unusually for train operators these days, up to two tandem bikes may use those four spaces instead. Reservation is compulsory, and a bike tag should be attached to each bike (get these at the ticket office). Voyager and Pendolino trains carry a yellow rectangle at the opposite end to the bike space.

Tip: to short-cut the automated telephone booking system, say 'agent' at the start. This puts you through to a real human being (albeit in a script-reading call centre) who is better able to help than the computer.

Arriva Trains Wales ☎ 0845 6061660, www.arrivatrainswales.co.uk, customer. relations@arrivatrainswales.co.uk

Covers W of the region

- Crewe to Manchester via Wilmslow

Reservations required.

East Coast Trains ☎ 08457 225111 (web support), 08457 225333 (customer services), www.eastcoast.co.uk,

East Coast's nearest station to the Peak District is Wakefield Westgate, but up to five bikes can be carried per train..

Included as their website is the only one that allows cycle reservations (for all train operating companies that take cycle reservations). Also groups of three to five cyclists travelling from London or Scotland may find the extra distance and changes involved in going by a route operated by East Coast Trains worthwhile to be together for the part of their journey that uses the East Coast line.

APPENDIX C
CAR PARKING

Visitors to the UK should be aware that parking in urban areas is strictly controlled. This can include:

- time-limited free parking (on-street or designated car parks)
- pay-and-display machine ticketed parking (on-street or designated car parks) at rates up to about £10 a day in urban areas
- complete parking restrictions denoted by yellow lines or signs only.

In all cases, the exact rules applying may only be discovered by reading obscure signs, and the rules may change in a very short distance! Failing to follow the rules can be an expensive mistake, punished by fixed fines or extortionate clamping/tow-away operators.

However, it is often possible to find free on-street parking close to many routes – just ensure that any vehicle is parked with consideration for those who live nearby (and have to put up with visitors invading their world every summer) and doesn't block any entranceway, driveway, road etc. Remember that farmers often need spontaneous access to apparently overgrown field entrances, and that agricultural vehicles may need a wide turning circle close to and opposite gates.

Car crime, usually meaning vehicle break-ins in pursuit of valuables, can be a minor problem, best avoided by following sound advice.

- Avoid leaving valuables (or simple evidence of a lot of luggage) on show.
- Car crime is generally worse closer to larger towns.

- Isolated locations are more risky – but remember to park considerately.
- 'Safe' daytime locations may become much worse overnight.

With very few exceptions, paying for parking does not guarantee immunity from crime.

Long Stay (for Route 21, the Tour de Peak District): parking for several nights is always going to be an issue in the Peak District, and this is especially so when leaving the car for a multiday cycle tour such as the Tour de Peak District. Secure long-stay parking in or around the Peak District is almost non-existent, and despite the difficulties of transporting cycles by train, taking the train to the start of any multiday route near or in the Peak District is usually the best option. However for those needing to arrive by car, the following advice may help.

The safest long term car park is in Derby City – Bold Lane Park Safe Car Park. It's record of zero thefts since 1998 speaks for itself, but it comes at a hefty price – 5 days, 4 nights will cost £98 (summer 2010 prices). However, it is one of the very few car parks in the whole of the UK that guarantees the safety of your vehicle and its contents from the moment you leave it, which may reassure those nervous about car crime. Outside this, probably the two best bets are the Brewery Street Car Park in Chesterfield, which is another reasonable long stay car park (max 7 days) that isn't expensive (£2 a day), or the Canal Street Car park in Whaley Bridge, which is free and allows long-term parking (overnight for several nights).

Most public car parks in the region are run by one of the National Park, local councils or private car parking companies. All have different policies about length and cost of stay, and any pre-purchase system they offer.

Peak District National Park Operated Car Parks

The following link gives information on the locations of PDNP operated car parks www.peakdistrict.gov.uk/index/visiting/parking/parking-locations.htm

The National Park operates an annual permit system which may be beneficial to those staying for more than a few days in the area: www.peakdistrict.gov.uk/index/visiting/parking.htm gives details of costs and how to apply for a permit (currently £30 for non residents).

The National Park area overlaps various local council areas. You'll generally find that in-town parking is operated by the local council, whereas nearby rural car parks are operated by the National Park.

Most of the area covered in this book is covered by Derbyshire Dales Council (south-east portion) and High Peak Council (north-west portion).

Derbyshire Dales Council

Derbyshire Dales Council (area roughly bounded by Matlock, Ashbourne and Bakewell) operates a similar but shorter scale parking permit system called a Rover Pass. These are available from local Tourist Information Centres or direct from the council. They last for three or seven consecutive days and can be used for parking on any of the council's car parks but they don't allow you to override any maximum period of stay at any car park!

For information on the locations of Derbyshire Dales Council's and other car parks in the Derbyshire Dales region visit www.derbyshiredales.gov.uk.

High Peak Council

High Peak Council (area roughly bounded by Buxton, Bamford and Glossop, www.highpeak.gov.uk) only offer three monthly parking season tickets. These will only be of use to the semi-permanent resident and information on council-operated and other car parks can be found on the website.

Other councils running roughly clockwise around the edges of the Peak District from the north include Kirklees, Barnsley, Sheffield, North-East Derbyshire, Chesterfield, Amber Valley, South Derbyshire, East Staffordshire, Staffordshire Moorlands, East Cheshire, Stockport, Tameside, Oldham.

Other parking information

Transport Direct www.transportdirect.info offers a parking search option for any town in Britain. Its search results list whether a car park has a parkmark or not (about the only level of security for car parks easily found on the internet).

APPENDIX D

REPAIR GUIDE

A crippling cycle breakdown can be very disheartening when its repair could be done simply with the correct tools, but there's always a balance to be struck against the weight of your toolkit. Punctures are by far the most likely cause of breakdown for a well maintained bike. The Peak District is quite densely populated for a national park, as well as being popular with visitors, so you will rarely be more than a kilometre or two from some form of assistance in the event of an unrepairable breakdown.

The first few items, marked with an asterisk below, should be considered essential for all rides, whereas the later items in the list are optional dependent on the route you are choosing (more useful on multi-day trips).

- Set of 3 **tyre levers***
- Spare **inner tube*** – of the same size and valve type as your tyres!
- **Pump*** Some pumps require a separate screw-on connector tube to connect to the valve on the tyre; there are two different types of connector for the two different valve types. Other pumps directly push onto the valve, and need to be partly dismantled to change between the two different valve types. Either way, make sure you can use your pump to inflate your tyres.
- **Puncture repair kit*** (in case you get more than one puncture) containing sandpaper, vulcanising solution and patches.
- **Spanner*** to enable wheels to be removed (if these are not quick-release).

- Tool to secure the clamps at the ends of brake and gear cables – usually a 5mm allen key.
- Tool to remove/replace/adjust brake pads – varies depending on brake type
- Tool to adjust saddle height, if not a quick release lever, and angle/fore-aft position – often a 6mm allen key
- Tool to laterally adjust V brakes – usually a screwdriver
- Tool to adjust derailer gears – usually a screwdriver
- Tool to tighten nuts securing luggage racks and mudguards – these can work loose very quickly under touring conditions
- Chain repair tool

Various all-in-one tools are available which combine a wide range of functions in a lightweight whole.

If you're riding with others, it can be tempting to save weight by sharing a toolkit, but remember that many of the items in the list may be specific to individual bikes.

Pre-ride checks for safety and enjoyment

These should all be repeated after a puncture has been repaired.

- Check that the tyres are sufficiently inflated – there should be no or little depression when a tyre tread is pushed firmly with the thumb. There should be minimal visible 'bulge' on firm level ground when loaded with the rider's weight.
- Observe that the alignment of each wheel is approximately centred in the frame/forks.

- Check, when pushing by the handlebars, that each brake will easily apply to lock the wheel with plenty of remaining travel of the lever.

- Gently lift the bike by the frame off the ground; if there is a slight clunking sensation that something is fractionally 'trying to stay behind', a wheel or the headset (handlebar) bearings may be loose. To tighten a wheel, see 'How to change an inner tube'; tightening headset bearings should only be attempted by the experienced.

- Lifted off the ground, spin each wheel to confirm that it turns without significant wobble, and without the brakes rubbing.

- Observe that the brake pads are not worn down below their minimum level, often indicated by visible ridges on their side.

- Observe that there is at least 2mm clearance between the tyre sidewalls and moving brake parts, with the brakes gently applied and all the way round each tyre.

- Check tyre treads and sidewalls for obvious glass, thorns, cuts or bulging out inner tube.

- Perform a short test ride to confirm that all gears can be selected without unreasonable effort, noise or loss of the chain

- Check that mudguards and luggage racks are rigidly attached, and that all their fixing screws are tight

How to change an inner tube

Although it is possible to repair a puncture while the wheel is attached to the bike, it's much easier done with the wheel off the bike. Better still, while out exchange the punctured tube for a spare inner tube and repair the puncture back at home.

1. Look/listen for evidence of where the puncture is – remember its position relative to the valve.

2. Cycles with wide tyres and rim-operated brakes may need the brakes temporarily releasing, and so incorporate a mechanism to disengage the brake cable without tools.

3. Turn the bike upside-down to stand on the saddle and handlebars, taking care not to damage any handlebar-mounted accessories.

4. Loosen the wheel (by quick release lever or loosening the wheel nuts on both sides if not quick release). With quick release levers it may be necessary to loosen the thumb wheel on the other end of the axle to allow it to fully release from the frame

5. Slide the wheel out of the frame and forks: wide tyres may need to be squeezed to pass between the brake pads.

6. Observe how the back wheel threads into the derailer and chain, and remember this for later.

7. Remove the valve cap and any knurled nut round the valve stem. Release any remaining air pressure.

8. Starting away from the valve position and then working towards the valve, use tyre levers to work one wall of the tyre out of the side of the wheel rim. Take care not to trap the tube as you do this. There is no need to fully remove the tyre from the wheel, just one sidewall.

9. Again starting away from the valve, pull the tube out from the tyre. Finishing at the valve, push the valve through the hole in the wheel rim to remove the inner tube.

10. Locate the cause of the puncture by inspection, or careful probing with fingertips. Remove the cause (usually glass or a thorn) so you don't get a repeat; the sharp end of a screwdriver or key can be useful to push it through the tread from the inside. Some 'inexplicable' punctures can be caused by hitting a sharp edged stone (resulting in a 'snakebite' pair of punctures), valve failure, or by sharp edges in the wheel inadequately protected by the rim tape. Remember there may be multiple punctures.

11. Now's the time to regret not carrying a spare tube – if so, go to 'How to repair a punctured inner tube'.

12. Slightly inflate the replacement tube so that it nearly holds its shape.

13. Reverse step 9 to put the tube back in the tyre and on the rim, starting with the valve.

14. Reverse step 8 to restore the tyre sidewall into the wheel rim, starting at the valve position. Take great care not to trap the tube between the wheel rim and tyre.

15. Re-fit any knurled nut onto the stem of the valve, inflate the tyre until firm and replace the valve cap.

16. Return the wheel into the cycle frame. Front wheels are usually oriented with the quick release lever on the left. Thread the back wheel back into the chain correctly. Take care not to dislodge brake pads, and that disc brakes locate correctly between the friction surfaces of the pads.

17. Secure the wheel. Quick release mechanisms will need the thumb wheel tightening until the lever can be turned through 180 degrees, offering very firm resistance towards the end of its travel. The quick release lever should end up firmly closed parallel and close to the cycle frame, but not touching it. Wheels with nuts should be tightened progressively on both sides.

18. Re-engage the brake cables if required.

19. Perform a full set of pre-ride checks.

How to repair a punctured inner tube

1. Inflate the tube to locate the puncture position, and mark it with a scratch or chalk.

2. Select a suitable sized repair patch.

3. Clean a generous area surrounding the hole using sandpaper.

4. Apply a small blob of vulcanising solution at the hole, and then quickly spread it out to form a thin film larger than the patch.

5. When the vulcanising solution has dried just enough to become tacky, peel the foil off the patch, and press it firmly down onto the centre of the hole. Press out from the centre to expel air bubbles and secure the edges. The paper/ plastic backing of the patch can remain in place.

6. Ideally leave the repair to cure for a few minutes before replacing on the wheel.

7. If you wish to test a newly repaired tube by inflation while still off the wheel, only do so with gentle pressure, as you may otherwise damage the new repair.

APPENDIX E – ROUTE SUMMARY TABLE

Route No	Grade	Start	To/Via
1	Easy	Chesterfield Station	Staveley
2	Easy	Carsington Water	Kirk Ireton
3	Easy	Ashopton	Ladybower
4	Easy	Middlewood Station	Lyme Park
5	Mod	Bamford Station	Ladybower
6	Mod	Ashbourne	Bradbourne
7	Mod	Chesterfield Station	Holymoorside
8	Mod	Tissington	Middleton via Youlgrave
9	Mod	Wirksworth	Hartington
10	Mod	Bakewell	Hartington
11	Mod	Leek	Roaches
12	Mod	Waterhouses	Morridge
13	Mod	Penistone Station	Holmefirth
14	Mod	Tideswell	Peak Forest
15	Hard	Buxton Station	Bakewell
16	Hard	Grindleford Station	Edale
17	Hard	Bamford Station	Mam Tor
18	Hard	Middlewood Station	Pym Chair
19	Hard	Marsden Station	Saddleworth Moor
20	Hard	Macclesfield Station	Roaches
21		TOUR DE PEAK DISTRICT	
Stage 1		Matlock Station	Dungworth
Stage 2		Dungworth	Marsden Station
Stage 3		Marsden Station	Whaley Bridge Station
Stage 4		Whaley Bridge Station	Blackshaw Moor
Stage 5		Blackshaw Moor	Matlock Station

Loop or Linear	Distance (Mi)	Distance (km)	Ascent (m)	Cycle Hire exists (Nearby – Y, Distant – N)	Page
Loop	11	18	190	N	33
Loop	8	13	250	Y	38
Loop	14	24	290	Y	43
Loop	12	20	335	N	48
Loop	11	18	290	Y	54
Loop	19	32	560	Y	59
Loop	18	30	480	N	64
Loop	28	47	990	N	70
Loop	28	47	865	Y	77
Loop	25	42	850	Y	84
Loop	26	43	990	N	90
Loop	26	44	820	Y	97
Loop	23	38	875	N	104
Loop	19	31	580	N	110
Loop	31	51	1050	N	117
Loop	35	59	1290	N	126
Loop	25	41	965	Y	135
Loop	22	37	900	N	143
Loop	29	48	1425	N	150
Loop	31	51	1225	N	158
TOUR DE PEAK DISTRICT					
Linear	31	51	1185	N	167
Linear	31	51	1290	N	175
Linear	31	51	1480	N	183
Linear	30	50	1220	N	193
Linear	32	53	1060	N	200

LISTING OF CICERONE GUIDES

BRITISH ISLES CHALLENGES, COLLECTIONS AND ACTIVITIES

The End to End Trail
The Mountains of England and Wales
1 Wales
2 England
The National Trails
The Relative Hills of Britain
The Ridges of England, Wales and Ireland
The UK Trailwalker's Handbook
Three Peaks, Ten Tors

MOUNTAIN LITERATURE

Unjustifiable Risk?

UK CYCLING

Border Country Cycle Routes
Cycling in the Peak District
Lands End to John O'Groats Cycle Guide
Mountain Biking in the Lake District
Mountain Biking on the South Downs
The Lancashire Cycleway

SCOTLAND

Backpacker's Britain
Central and Southern Scottish Highlands
Northern Scotland
Ben Nevis and Glen Coe
North to the Cape
Not the West Highland Way
Scotland's Best Small Mountains
Scotland's Far West
Scotland's Mountain Ridges
Scrambles in Lochaber
The Border Country
The Central Highlands
The Great Glen Way
The Isle of Mull
The Isle of Skye
The Pentland Hills: A Walker's Guide
The Southern Upland Way

The Speyside Way
The West Highland Way
Walking in Scotland's Far North
Walking in the Cairngorms
Walking in the Hebrides
Walking in the Ochils, Campsie Fells and Lomond Hills
Walking in Torridon
Walking Loch Lomond and the Trossachs
Walking on Harris and Lewis
Walking on Jura, Islay and Colonsay
Walking on the Isle of Arran
Walking on the Orkney and Shetland Isles
Walking the Galloway Hills
Walking the Lowther Hills
Walking the Munros
1 Southern, Central and Western Highlands
2 Northern Highlands and the Cairngorms
Winter Climbs Ben Nevis and Glen Coe
Winter Climbs in the Cairngorms
World Mountain Ranges: Scotland

NORTHERN ENGLAND TRAILS

A Northern Coast to Coast Walk
Backpacker's Britain Northern England
Hadrian's Wall Path
The Dales Way
The Pennine Way
The Spirit of Hadrian's Wall

NORTH EAST ENGLAND, YORKSHIRE DALES AND PENNINES

Historic Walks in North Yorkshire
South Pennine Walks
The Cleveland Way and the Yorkshire Wolds Way

The North York Moors
The Reivers Way
The Teesdale Way
The Yorkshire Dales Angler's Guide
The Yorkshire Dales North and East South and West
Walking in County Durham
Walking in Northumberland
Walking in the North Pennines
Walking in the Wolds
Walks in Dales Country
Walks in the Yorkshire Dales
Walks on the North York Moors Books 1 and 2

NORTH WEST ENGLAND AND THE ISLE OF MAN

A Walker's Guide to the Lancaster Canal
Historic Walks in Cheshire
Isle of Man Coastal Path
The Isle of Man
The Ribble Way
Walking in Lancashire
Walking in the Forest of Bowland and Pendle
Walking on the West Pennine Moors
Walks in Lancashire Witch Country
Walks in Ribble Country
Walks in Silverdale and Arnside
Walks in the Forest of Bowland

LAKE DISTRICT

Coniston Copper Mines
Great Mountain Days in the Lake District
Lake District Winter Climbs
Lakeland Fellranger
The Central Fells
The Mid-Western Fells
The Near Eastern Fells
The North-Western Wells
The Southern Fells
The Western Fells

Roads and Tracks of the
Lake District
Rocky Rambler's Wild Walks
Scrambles in the Lake District
North
South
Short Walks in Lakeland
1 South Lakeland
2 North Lakeland
3 West Lakeland
The Cumbria Coastal Way
The Cumbria Way and the
Allerdale Ramble
The Lake District
Anglers' Guide
Tour of the Lake District

DERBYSHIRE, PEAK DISTRICT AND MIDLANDS

High Peak Walks
The Star Family Walks
Walking in Derbyshire
White Peak Walks
The Northern Dales
The Southern Dales

SOUTHERN ENGLAND

A Walker's Guide to the
Isle of Wight
London – The definitive
walking guide
The Cotswold Way
The Greater Ridgeway
The Lea Valley Walk
The North Downs Way
The South Downs Way
The South West Coast Path
The Thames Path
Walking in Bedfordshire
Walking in Berkshire
Walking in Buckinghamshire
Walking in Kent
Walking in Sussex
Walking in the Isles of Scilly
Walking in the Thames Valley
Walking on Dartmoor
Walking on Guernsey
Walking on Jersey
Walks in the South Downs
National Park

WALES AND WELSH BORDERS

Backpacker's Britain
Wales
Glyndwr's Way
Great Mountain Days in
Snowdonia
Hillwalking in Snowdonia
Hillwalking in Wales
Vols 1 and 2
Offa's Dyke Path
Ridges of Snowdonia
Scrambles in Snowdonia
The Ascent of Snowdon
The Lleyn Peninsula
Coastal Path
The Pembrokeshire
Coastal Path
The Shropshire Hills
The Spirit Paths of Wales
Walking in Pembrokeshire
Walking on the
Brecon Beacons
Welsh Winter Climbs

INTERNATIONAL CHALLENGES, COLLECTIONS AND ACTIVITIES

Canyoning
Europe's High Points

EUROPEAN CYCLING

Cycle Touring in France
Cycle Touring in Ireland
Cycle Touring in Spain
Cycle Touring in Switzerland
Cycling in the French Alps
Cycling the Canal du Midi
Cycling the River Loire
The Danube Cycleway
The Grand Traverse of the
Massif Central
The Way of St James

AFRICA

Climbing in the Moroccan
Anti-Atlas
Kilimanjaro:
A Complete Trekker's Guide
Mountaineering in the
Moroccan High Atlas
Trekking in the Atlas Mountains
Walking in the Drakensberg

ALPS – CROSS-BORDER ROUTES

100 Hut Walks in the Alps
Across the Eastern Alps: E5
Alpine Ski Mountaineering
1 Western Alps
2 Central and Eastern Alps
Chamonix to Zermatt
Snowshoeing
Tour of Mont Blanc
Tour of Monte Rosa
Tour of the Matterhorn
Trekking in the Alps
Walking in the Alps
Walks and Treks in the
Maritime Alps

PYRENEES AND FRANCE/ SPAIN CROSS-BORDER ROUTES

Rock Climbs In The Pyrenees
The GR10 Trail
The Mountains of Andorra
The Pyrenean Haute Route
The Pyrenees
The Way of St James
France and Spain
Through the Spanish Pyrenees:
GR11
Walks and Climbs in
the Pyrenees

AUSTRIA

Trekking in Austria's
Hohe Tauern
Trekking in the Stubai Alps
Trekking in the Zillertal Alps
Walking in Austria

EASTERN EUROPE

The High Tatras
The Mountains of Romania
Walking in Bulgaria's
National Parks
Walking in Hungary

FRANCE

Ecrins National Park
GR20: Corsica
Mont Blanc Walks
Mountain Adventures in
the Maurienne
The Cathar Way

The GR5 Trail
The Robert Louis
   Stevenson Trail
Tour of the Oisans: The GR54
Tour of the Queyras
Tour of the Vanoise
Trekking in the Vosges and Jura
Vanoise Ski Touring
Walking in Provence
Walking in the Cathar Region
Walking in the Cevennes
Walking in the Dordogne
Walking in the Haute Savoie
   North and South
Walking in the Languedoc
Walking in the Tarentaise and
   Beaufortain Alps
Walking on Corsica

GERMANY
Germany's Romantic Road
Walking in the Bavarian Alps
Walking in the Harz Mountains
Walking the River Rhine Trail

HIMALAYA
Annapurna:
   A Trekker's Guide
Bhutan
Everest: A Trekker's Guide
Garhwal and Kumaon: A
   Trekker's and Visitor's Guide
Kangchenjunga:
   A Trekker's Guide
Langtang with Gosainkund and
   Helambu: A Trekker's Guide
Manaslu: A Trekker's Guide
The Mount Kailash Trek

IRELAND
Irish Coastal Walks
The Irish Coast to Coast Walk
The Mountains of Ireland

ITALY
Gran Paradiso
Italy's Sibillini National Park
Shorter Walks in the Dolomites
Through the Italian Alps
Trekking in the Apennines
Trekking in the Dolomites
Via Ferratas of the Italian
   Dolomites: Vols 1 and 2

Walking in Sicily
Walking in the
   Central Italian Alps
Walking in the Dolomites
Walking in Tuscany
Walking on the Amalfi Coast

MEDITERRANEAN
Jordan – Walks, Treks, Caves,
   Climbs and Canyons
The Ala Dag
The High Mountains of Crete
The Mountains of Greece
Treks and Climbs in Wadi Rum,
   Jordan
Walking in Malta
Western Crete

NORTH AMERICA
British Columbia
The Grand Canyon
The John Muir Trail
The Pacific Crest Trail

SOUTH AMERICA
Aconcagua and the
   Southern Andes
Hiking and Biking Peru's
   Inca Trails
Torres del Paine

SCANDINAVIA
Trekking in Greenland
Walking in Norway

**SLOVENIA, CROATIA AND
MONTENEGRO**
The Julian Alps of Slovenia
The Mountains of Montenegro
Trekking in Slovenia
Walking in Croatia

SPAIN AND PORTUGAL
Costa Blanca Walks
   1 West and 2 East
Mountain Walking in
   Southern Catalunya
The Mountains of Central Spain
Trekking through Mallorca
Via de la Plata
Walking in Madeira
Walking in Mallorca
Walking in the Algarve

Walking in the Canary Islands
   2 East
Walking in the
   Cordillera Cantabrica
Walking in the Sierra Nevada
Walking on La Gomera and
   El Hierro
Walking on La Palma
Walking the GR7 in Andalucia
Walks and Climbs in the
   Picos de Europa

SWITZERLAND
Alpine Pass Route
Central Switzerland
The Bernese Alps
Tour of the Jungfrau Region
Walking in the Valais
Walking in Ticino
Walks in the Engadine

TECHNIQUES
Geocaching in the UK
Indoor Climbing
Lightweight Camping
Map and Compass
Mountain Weather
Moveable Feasts
Rock Climbing
Sport Climbing
The Book of the Bivvy
The Hillwalker's Guide to
   Mountaineering
The Hillwalker's Manual

MINI GUIDES
Avalanche!
Navigating with a GPS
Navigation
Pocket First Aid and
   Wilderness Medicine
Snow

For full information on all our
guides, and to order books and
eBooks, visit our website:
www.cicerone.co.uk.

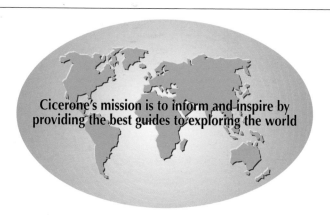

Cicerone's mission is to inform and inspire by providing the best guides to exploring the world

Since its foundation 40 years ago, Cicerone has specialised in publishing guidebooks and has built a reputation for quality and reliability. It now publishes nearly 300 guides to the major destinations for outdoor enthusiasts, including Europe, UK and the rest of the world.

Written by leading and committed specialists, Cicerone guides are recognised as the most authoritative. They are full of information, maps and illustrations so that the user can plan and complete a successful and safe trip or expedition – be it a long face climb, a walk over Lakeland fells, an alpine cycling tour, a Himalayan trek or a ramble in the countryside.

With a thorough introduction to assist planning, clear diagrams, maps and colour photographs to illustrate the terrain and route, and accurate and detailed text, Cicerone guides are designed for ease of use and access to the information.

If the facts on the ground change, or there is any aspect of a guide that you think we can improve, we are always delighted to hear from you.

Cicerone Press
2 Police Square Milnthorpe Cumbria LA7 7PY
Tel: 015395 62069 Fax: 015395 63417
info@cicerone.co.uk www.cicerone.co.uk

CICERONE